Head of itinerant preacher, Afghanistan

GYPSIES
AN ILLUSTRATED HISTORY

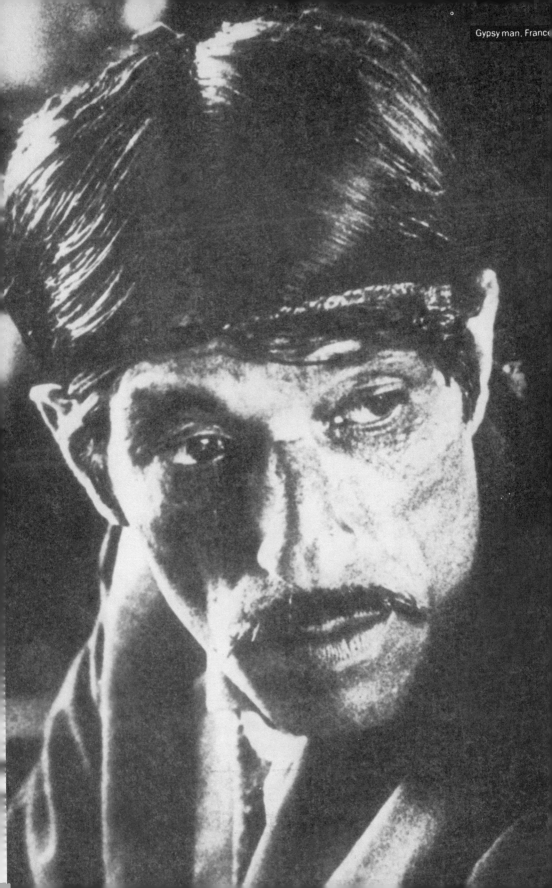

Gypsy woman. Greece

BY JEAN-PIERRE LIEGEOIS

Gypsies on the move, Spain

SAQI BOOKS

Gypsy caravan, France

TRANSLATED BY
TONY BERRETT

PHOTOGRAPHS

Silvester/Rapho (front cover, pages 2, 3, 4-5, 6-7, 8-9, 20-1, 43, 79, 80-1, 114-15, 142, 153, 166);

Giraudon (1); Denis Harvey (10-11, 126-7, 128-9, 133, 137); Ficowski (12); Jean Vertut (26-7); J-P. Liégeois (31, 172); Holmes-Lebel (32); Bibliothèque Nationale (39, 40, 91, 98-9, 102, 103); Musée de

En route to a Gypsy gathering, France

l'homme (46); Dolly Schmidt (48, 60-1, 62, 119, 122, 182-3); Gérard Rondeau (52-3, 158-9, 176-7, 185); Marcelle Vallet (55, 59); Philippe Lemaire de Marne (65); J. Leonard Amaya (66, 69, 72, 73, 74, 75); Marbeuf (70-1); Gemeentelijk Museum Roermond (86); Lucien Clergue (148-9); Roger Viollet (161).

CONTENTS

Introduction **13**
1. Origins **17**
2. Gypsy Society **49**
3. Gypsies and Non-Gypsies **87**
4. Changing Times **143**
5. The Twilight of the Gypsies? **173**
Bibliography **186**

Vickers trailer at fair, England

Bear-leaders, Yugoslavia

The publishers gratefully acknowledge the assistance of
Thomas Acton and Donald Kenrick in the preparation of this volume.

British Library Cataloguing-in-Publication Data
A catalogue record for this book is available from the British Library

ISBN 0 86356 554 9
EAN 9-780863-565540

This English translation is based on *Tsiganes*,
La Découverte, 1983. ©Jean-Pierre Liégeois, 1983 and 2005.
Many of the photographs in this volume previously
appeared in *Les Tsiganes*, Editions du Seuil, 1971.
First published in 1986 by Saqi Books.
This edition published 2005.

SAQI
26 Westbourne Grove, London W2 5RH
www.saqibooks.com

INTRODUCTION

Gypsies are misunderstood, partly because of their own characteristics and partly because of the attitudes of those around them. Most people who come into contact with Gypsies know nothing of where they come from, misjudge their customs, and, in their ignorance, project their own anxieties and desires. The result is a body of stereotyped images, sometimes centuries old, but all too often taken as reality by non-Gypsies. The Gypsies themselves—scattered and diverse, with no territory and few written records of their own—tend to rely on invisibility, for experience has taught them that if they stand out they suffer rejection and punishment, and if they cling too closely to someone or something they will lose their prime tactic of day-to-day survival: to bend in order not to break. When they do appear openly, it is in necessarily disguised ways, as performers and fortune-tellers, as what others expect them to be. And the people of each nation probably know more about small groups living on the other side of the earth than they do about the often numerous Gypsy populations who live and move among them.

The populations that non-Gypsies call 'Gypsy' actually constitute a rich mosaic of ethnic fragments, very different groups going under different names: Kalderaš, Lovari, Sinti, Manuš, Romanichals, Kalé, and others. 'Gypsy' is not a Gypsy word, and all these various groups distinguish themselves sharply from one another. Given this diversity, it is not easy to give a single description that embraces the multiplicity of groups and their points of view. Most portrayals of Gypsies have therefore been slanted, generalizing to Gypsies as a whole things that are typical of only one group, or suggesting that the group being discussed constitutes the only real Gypsies, the others being somehow 'less Gypsy', or presenting Gypsies as a homogeneous whole. And these errors, of course, are not mutually exclusive.

An overall presentation is therefore difficult, for the particular and the general pull in different directions, and in the eyes of both Gypsies and attentive observers it is the particular that counts. But it would take many volumes to study all these different populations, and the general and common features are also crucial if there is to be any synthesis. Anyone writing about Gypsies runs the risk of being too simple for specialists and too detailed for readers new to the subject.

Yet this book is deliberately meant to be an overall and general work. While it may well suffer from the intrinsic defects of this kind of approach (in particular, there is the danger of encouraging the reader to generalize too much), I hope that it also has some of its advantages—giving a clear survey of the field, for example.

Once we rule out comprehensiveness, we are left with what is essential. In the chapter on culture (chapter 2), for example, I will not go through all the infinitely variable rituals (of marriage, justice, festivals, and so on), but will concentrate on the *spirit* in which these rituals do or do not take place. I have chosen to try to express the spirit rather than the details of Gypsy culture partly because the Gypsies themselves prefer not to expose the intimate features of an often misunderstood culture which they have no wish to see vulgarized or besmirched.

The book has three main aims. First, it attempts both to demonstrate the existence of Gypsy culture and to bring out its essence.

Second, it calls attention to the denial of this culture, and of the people in whom it is embodied, by states, local authorities and populations, who have been pursuing policies of rejection or assimilation for centuries. Gypsy populations cannot be understood without studying the people they live among. This will tell us much about the Gypsies' environment, and, however diverse Gypsy populations may be, perceptions of them and the sort of reactions they arouse are similar everywhere. State policies are equivalent throughout Western Europe. In the 1980s, as governments contemplate measures which purport to show respect for Gypsies and Travellers, it is useful to draw the lessons of a past that is still very much alive.

Finally, the book tries to show that Gypsy culture is neither unchanging nor passive. In every age the struggle against prevailing policies has produced day-to-day strategies of adaptation, and recent years have seen the rise of Gypsy organizations with national and international ramifications. The birth of Gypsy power has upset state policies towards Gypsies and represents a break with the tradition of invisibility, flexibility, and diversity of the many Gypsy groups.

I would hope, too, that the Gypsy example will encourage readers to think about the more general problem of relations between minorities and the states in which they live. The case of the Gypsies is especially revealing of attitudes and forms of behaviour towards people whose culture is different, for the Gypsy populations—considered as of no consequence in every respect and so far lacking the will or means to respond—have allowed others to act unimpeded, to project their desires and stereotypes freely.

Gypsy groups have never abandoned their belief in their own worth. Today they are reaching the end of their tether. Caught in an inextricable web of state regulations that draw them out of their own world towards assimilation into other populations, they live in a state of growing impoverishment, deprivation, and violence, conditions which they had previously managed to avoid. It is vitally important to grasp the quality of their existence and to take account of the justice of their demands. Perhaps better understanding will produce greater respect.

A brief note on some spellings and terminology. In the Gypsy words used in this book, the unfamiliar letters are pronounced as follows:

č   is like the *ch* in *check*
j   is like the *y* in *young*
š   is like the *sh* in *shall*
ž   is like the *s* in *pleasure*
dž is like the *dg* in *budget*.

The name of the Gypsy language is 'Romany', which is also used as an adjective referring to Gypsy institutions (as: 'Romany League').

There is no single word for 'Gypsy' in all Romany dialects. In some dialects, the word 'Rom' is a noun meaning 'Gypsy', its plural being 'Roma'. But not all Gypsies call themselves Roma, and to complicate matters there is a sub-group of Gypsies who do call themselves Rom (in the singular and plural alike), but use the designation to set themselves off from other Gypsy groups (such as the Sinti, for example). This confusion, unfortunately, is inescapable, for it is both a reflection and a consequence of Gypsy diversity. Nor can the problem be surmounted by abandoning the word 'Gypsy' in favour of 'Traveller', 'nomad', or any other 'non-ethnic' generic term. However well intentioned, such labels have the effect of characterizing Gypsies by some particular feature of their life-style; precisely by avoiding any 'ethnic' content, these labels effectively deny the existence of a specifically Gypsy culture.

In this book, therefore, the word 'Gypsy' is used to refer to the whole mosaic of Romany peoples and their culture. Where appropriate and not misleading, the terms Rom and Roma have been used as well. Finally, although there is no single and universal Romany term for 'Gypsy', there is such a term for *non-*Gypsy. Although the spelling varies in different Romany dialects, a standard one has been used here throughout, a form that would be recognizable to any Gypsy: a non-Gypsy is a *gadžo* (plural: *gadže*).

1

ORIGINS

Anyone who has never looked closely at the wanderings and tribulations of the Gypsies might well wonder whether they have a history at all. People are generally ignorant of where they come from and know even less about how they got where they are now. Gypsies are disparate in so many ways, are so widely separated from one another by distance and differing customs, that it may well be wondered whether they are a single people or just a profusion of groups from different homelands linked by certain similarities that make them comparable. Do they all come originally from the same place? When did they first appear? These and many other questions have long been asked. Some remain unanswered.

Over the past two centuries history, anthropology, and linguistics have made it possible to retrace part of the history of this people with no written language, an achievement that seemed doubtful not so long ago, for the simple reason that the Gypsies have no archives, and indeed have few written records at all. Therein lies one of the obstacles facing anyone who wants to examine the available information. Researchers move in shifting territory, for precious little of the documentation is of Gypsy provenance; everything is written by others who may have made mistakes, left things out (whether deliberately or by accident), exaggerated or underestimated. Moreover, translations and the many transcriptions of documents are marred by important errors. There is also the problem of the variety of names of the population groups being described. Each nation, even each region, uses more than one term to designate the same Gypsy groups, and also uses these same terms to describe other groups.

In this context, many different theories have been advanced, often based purely on imagination, buttressed by the few elements that may provide some real hints: the language in which Gypsies communicate, 'incomprehensible' to others; the 'oral tradition', or body of stories and legends handed down from generation to generation or made up to answer the prying questions of the curious; the songs, dances, clothes, and astonishing rituals, sometimes frightening for non-Gypsies—and all of this embellished by the state of mind characteristic of each age, spiced with a dash of romanticism. One more or less representative feature of some particular nomadic group would become the foundation for an entire theory. It was all a lot of fun. That is one reason why it took so long to get down to the more prosaic considerations of reliable research. Alleged facts that feed prejudice and stereotypes always spread faster than the findings of research.

Legends

It was legend that gave rise to most of the hypotheses, which were sometimes later taken as certainties. From the very first appearance of Gypsies, there were people who tried to find out about their legends and commit them to writing. But were some of these legends perhaps misinterpreted? When did they arise? And in what circumstances? Gypsies have often protected themselves from unwelcome inquiries by deceiving their questioners, by inventing stories to explain and facilitate their nomadism. Moreover, the earliest legends were influenced by other traditions. Some stories, for example, make use of elements of Christian tradition to explain the curse said to hang over Gypsies and to condemn them to perpetual wandering. One of the most striking legends tells of the Crucifixion. The ancestors of the Gypsies, it says, forged the nails used to crucify Christ; three of these were used, but the fourth, a red-hot piece of iron, has followed them and their descendants everywhere: they are unable to cool it or to escape it.

There are many versions of this legend. Some Kalderaš

Gypsies in the suburbs of Lyons in France say that a Gypsy blacksmith forged twelve nails to crucify three men; but then, thinking that three was 'a sign of blessing', he hid one nail, telling himself that the man crucified with only three nails would be 'the man of the blessing'. He was thus able to identify and follow the *Sunto Del* (Holy God), to associate himself with Him and thus to enter paradise [14].* Some Gypsies in Serbia believe that their ancestors stole the fourth nail from the cross and that they were therefore condemned to wander for seven years or seven centuries. Others say that the Gypsies were Christ's guards but that they got drunk and were unable to defend him; yet others that they were punished for refusing to shelter the Virgin and Child during their flight from Egypt. In fact, the Gypsies did not reach Palestine until several centuries after Christ.

When they first arrived in Western Europe, many Gypsies said that the Pope, who had declared them apostates from the Christian faith, had ordered them to do seven years of penance. Is this pure legend, or is there some truth in it? What appear to be authentic papal letters have been discovered and 'it is quite possible that some tribes, who had become Christians in the Byzantine Empire, found themselves by turns under the rule of the Cross and the Crescent during the wars with the Muslims' [129, p. 17]. This account, many versions of which are found, is thus not pure fantasy.

Another legend has it that the Gypsies are the descendants of Adam and a first woman created before Eve; they were therefore born without original sin and, unlike the rest of mankind, are not condemned to work or to suffer other punishments. There are other creative explanations of nomadism too. When an early-sixteenth-century author asked some Gypsies why they never stopped wandering, he was told that 'the road was closed to them, which prevented them from returning to their country even though the term of their penance was over' [82]. Another story illustrates the combination of various traditions. It relates that the ancestors of the Gypsies—then just one tribe among others, but unusually intelligent and bold—sought to become

* The numbers in square brackets refer to the bibliography at the end of the book.

19

Village Gypsies, Spain ▷

the most powerful group, making war on other peoples. At one point in their attack, they had to cross the salt-sea, the *Porsaida*. The waters parted at an invocation of their leader, but then engulfed them in the middle of their crossing. Only a few men survived and were condemned to a life of wandering [14, pp. 22–72]. A nineteenth-century German author reports a similar tale.

According to another legend, the original homeland of the Gypsies was in eastern India: the Gond are a people known in Nepal and Burma, and one of their branches, the Gond Sindhu or Sinti, is said to have set out westward, crossing out of India. They domesticated the horse and then headed for Chaldea, where they taught yoga, dangerous acrobatics, how to walk through fire, and many other feats; they were warmly welcomed because of their skill in carving bronze and gold. In Chaldea they devised the science of the stars, and then some of them set out with Abraham to the land of Canaan. They finally arrived in Egypt, performed their feats for the pharaohs, and were allowed to stay. According to this legend, then, the Sinti group of Gypsies moved from east to west, from India to Egypt. But there are many other tales. One legend, for instance, recalling the prophecy of Ezekiel 'I shall scatter the Egyptians among the nations', ascribes an Egyptian origin to the Gypsies: when Pharaoh's army was engulfed in the waters during the crossing of the Red Sea, one young man and one young woman escaped, and they became the Adam and Eve of the Gypsies [26, p. 20].

These few legends show the variety of notions of Gypsy origins. There are a few common themes: we begin to get the idea that the Gypsies are a people of remote ancestry who have a common history—or at least some groups do, for the legends sometimes diverge. Among the many countries, mythical or real, mentioned in these tales, those lying between India and Egypt stand out most often as the site of the Gypsies' entrance on to the stage of history. Finally, we can detect diverse influences: the impact of belated conversion to Christianity on a history built of memories of distant events, the addition of disparate elements during the trek across various countries, and the integration of these new elements, tailored to suit Gypsy taste and reinterpreted by the people telling the tales.

Strange Hypotheses and Reasonable Guesses

Even in the best of cases, hypotheses about Gypsy origins are reflections of Gypsy legends on which theories are built. In the other cases, random structures are concocted out of wholly gratuitous assertions of myths that have nothing to do with Gypsies at all. Most of the hypotheses are no less fabulous than the legends.

In 1841 Predari opined that the Gypsies were none other than the descendants of a prehistoric people who had been turned into nomads by a 'geological or political' catastrophe and had been roaming far and wide ever since [94]. In 1844 Bataillard wrote that Gypsies, blacksmiths in the Bronze Age, 'may have established their production centres in the region of the western Alps; from there, trading as they roamed, they spread their metalworking among the Celts and other tribes' [8]. This thesis, although far from easy to support, was taken up by others. 'It seems certain', Franz de Ville wrote, 'that it was the Gypsies who introduced bronze into Europe.' Many hypotheses present the Gypsies as the inventors or propagators of bronze, or attribute their origin and dispersion to the art of metalworking, in turn linked to magic and witchcraft. This has the advantage of accounting simultaneously for their performances as musicians and singers, for example, and for the way other peoples treated them.

Enea Silvio Piccolomini, who later became Pope Pius II, thought that the Gypsies were descendants of a people from the Caucasus; others claimed that they had lived in the Camargue for two thousand years; and yet others that they lived 'on the borders of Turkey and Hungary' [28, 65]. A few biblical allusions that might possibly refer to the Gypsies have also been picked up. It has been said that some groups of Gypsies are descendants of Jews [91, 136]. The Gitanos were believed to be descended from Andalusian Moors, or from a mixed race of Jews and Moors born of the migration of these two peoples following their expulsion from Spain after the *Reconquista*. In one of his *Discursos* (1619) Sancho de Moncada describes the Gitanos as a collection of layabouts and outlaws, members of the 'sect of Gitanismo' [12]. Some claimed that they came from the

Iberian peninsula, arguing that they were also called Cingaros, from the name Cinga (now El Cinca), a stream in the province of Huesca. Others said that they were called Cingaros because they were led by a captain called Cingo, and still others that they were called Cingalos or Cingaros because they acted like the *cinclo*, a wandering and anxious bird that settles in the nests of others.

In the sixteenth century, the French scholar Pierre Belon held that the Gypsies, treated as foreigners in Egypt just as they were everywhere else, came from Walachia, while in the same era Bonaventura Vulcanius had them coming from Nubia. This was also the view of the seventeenth-century Dutch Calvinist theologian Gisbertus Voetius. Father Garassus, also in the seventeenth century, thought they came from the Pyrenees: 'It has been discovered that they are rabble gathered from the vicinity of Béarn, Biscay and the land of Labour, and their language indeed demonstrates this, as does the custom of several French provinces in which these idlers are called Biscayans' [12, 135, 134, 44]. In 1857 J.-A. Vaillant, a professor of literature in Romania, asserted in *Les Rômes, histoire vraie des vrais Bohémiens* that the 'Rômes' had invented the Gospel more than ten centuries before Christ. 'I have succeeded', he wrote, 'in unravelling the knot of the ages, and I will put my finger on the true origins of the things of this world.' The Rômes, he said, stand at the origin of the civilizations of Egypt, Greece, Italy and the Gauls, and of the East as well [122].

In 1973 Jean-Claude Frère, ignoring twentieth-century historians of the Gypsies, explained in *L'Enigme des Gitans* that although they 'are now called Gypsies [Gitans], for centuries, under various names, they stood at the origin of all our great civilizations, in Judaea, Egypt, Greece, Rome'. The author, 'through patient research, has established beyond doubt that the founders of the traditional great civilizations belonged to the race that came to be called Gitans [Gypsies] in the sixteenth century of our era' [43]. A century earlier, the more careful Baudrimont believed that 'the ancestors of the Gypsies lived in Babylon, whose destruction condemned them to exodus' [10]. Blaise Cendrars thought he could trace the Gypsies to the Guanches of the Canary Islands, supposedly the sole survivors of Atlantis. The Marquis de Baroncelli, a friend of many Gypsies, invited Colonel Buffalo Bill Cody to the Camargue to compare the Gypsies with Sioux and Iroquois. Cody discovered striking resemblances in colour, type, customs, and vocabulary. These 'support the hypothesis of a dark-red-skinned race of nomads who followed the setting sun and who were decimated by the sinking of Atlantis in the Stone or Bronze Age. The survivors of the catastrophe on the eastern slope were the fellahin who surged into Egypt, the Gypsies . . . and the Basques' [123].

One of the most elaborate and widespread hypotheses gave an origin in or near Egypt. This has been the position of Spaniards in particular. One version of this theory is found in José Carlos de Luna's *Gitanos de la Bética* [73]: during the twelfth and fourteenth dynasties of ancient Egypt, anarchy lay over the country. It was a time of turmoil and civil war. Towards 1778 BC Egypt was invaded by the Hyksos, 'shepherd kings' from Asia, who arrived with horses and war chariots and occupied the Nile valley. Only much later (under the eighteenth dynasty) was the country liberated. The Gypsies are the descendants of these Hyksos, who introduced the horse into Egypt and may have established settlements along the Spanish coast at the same time as the Greek and Phoenician colonies.

What observations led some people to persist with a theory of Egyptian origin even after it had been shown that Gypsies spoke an Indian language? First and most obviously there are the names. When they first appeared, the Gypsies called themselves and were called Egyptians. Their leaders often claimed to be counts of Egypt, or of Little Egypt. The tales they told were of Egypt. In several countries they are still known by names derived from 'Egypt': Gitanos in Spain, Gypsies in England, Egyptiers and Gyptenaers in the Netherlands, Evgjit in Albania, Yifti in Greece. There is one common tale very similar to José Carlos de Luna's hypothesis: the Gypsies fled Egypt pursued by the Egyptians, and many drowned crossing a river. The survivors escaped over a bridge they had built of reeds. Ever since, they have regarded the reed as a symbol of their liberation, and story-tellers carry a strip of reed as an amulet [110]. This presumed origin is said to be reflected in some aspects of Gypsy life. Songs in particular refer to it, and according to the Spanish

The Hyksos: ancestors of the Gypsies? (Tomb of Rekmire, Thebes, Egypt)

musicologist Felipe Pedrell, in Gitano songs, 'popularized by the people, and surviving only in Andalusia, there are elements that trace the origin of this once-nomadic people back to ancient Egypt' [cf. 75]. Some aspects of Gypsy songs—like guitars and castanets—can be seen in Egyptian bas-reliefs, and the words of the songs themselves, with their exaltation of 'brown' over 'white', pour scorn over everything Western. Some flamenco ballads may well have come from the Song of Songs [73, 26].

At the beginning of the eighteenth century, Mathurin La Croze, an inquiring scholar and polyglot, found a few words he thought were Gypsy in a study of the language and history of the Ethiopians [quoted in 129, p. 193]. José Carlos de Luna's hypothesis found many supporters; Lafuente, for example, deals with it at length [65, pp 168–80]. Voltaire devoted a chapter of his *Essai sur les moeurs* to the 'Bohemians or Egyptians'. He believed they were 'remnants of those ancient priests and priestesses of Isis, intermixed with those of the goddess of Syria . . . Their castanets and Basque drums are the cymbals and crotala of the priests of Isis and Syria.' Other scholars, such as Court de Gébelin in 1781 and Samuel Roberts in 1836, also upheld an Egyptian origin [Gébelin, see 129, pp. 40–1 and 184; Roberts, 101].

But far too many facts weigh against all theories of Egyptian origin. To begin with, there is the meaning of the word 'Egypt' at the time the Gypsies arrived in Western Europe. Two Alsatian chroniclers, Daniel Specklin and Jacques Trausch, wrote that at the beginning of the fifteenth century 'the first Gypsies arrived in Strasburg and throughout the country. There were some fourteen thousand of them [*an exaggerated figure*—J.-P.L.] scattered here and there. They said they had to wander for seven years doing penance. They came from Epirus, which the common man calls Little Egypt.' The explanation may be that in medieval Europe the whole eastern Mediterranean, including Syria, Greece, Cyprus, and neighbouring lands, was known as Little Egypt. The Turks also called the region of Izmir (formerly Nicodemia) 'Little Egypt', because of its fertility. And well before the arrival of the Gypsies in Europe, 'all highway mountebanks and tricksters' were dubbed 'Egyptians' [26, p. 20]. In 1540 the scholar Lorenzo Palmireno observed that the Gitans did not understand 'Egyptian' but used 'vernacular Greek' [86, p. 36]. Far more interesting is the observation of Eric O. Winsted: at the end of the fifteenth century German travellers mention two or three hundred Gypsy huts in Modon in the Peloponnese, at the foot of Mount Gype, better known by Venetian colonists as Little Egypt [141; see also 55]. Furthermore, Spanish archives indicate that the Gypsies arrived in 1425 from the north, in other words from France, and not after a frequently cited but none the less hypothetical journey through North Africa [5].

Other hypotheses emerged from linguistic studies. There is mention of their language from the very first appearance of Gypsies in Europe. Most authors called it an incomprehensible jargon, a kind of perverted slang. Sebastian Münster, an early-sixteeth-century geographer, got interested in the Gypsies' knack for languages and devoted a chapter of his *Cosmographia Universalis* to them, but he saw their language as nothing more than a mishmash: 'They have created a jargon of their own, yet they draw upon all the languages of Europe.' It was a long time before it was realized that there was a real Gypsy language. One of the first to take an interest in it was Bonaventura Vulcanius, whose book included a glossary of more than seventy words, supplied by Joseph Scaliger, a teacher at Agen [see 82, 135, 32]. Although Vulcanius was unaware of the origin of the language, he deserves credit for bringing it into the field of research. In 1542 another scholar, Andrew Borde, published a short 'manual' with sentences in many languages, including Romany [19; see also 30 and 129, p. 43]. The frequency in these vocabularies of words relating to drinking and inns—the most fully conjugated verb in Vulcanius's work is the verb 'to drink'—suggests that these scholars did their research by going to public houses with Gypsies to learn the current vocabulary.

Studies of the Gypsy language remained stagnant for two centuries. But later, as methods were increasingly refined, it finally became possible to locate the country of origin of this language: India. This is now a certainty, which leads immediately to many fresh suppositions and suggests answers to some outstanding questions. Are all Gypsies from India? Why did they leave, and when? Documents are few and far between; only two pieces of literary evidence are worth examining.

The first comes from the Persian poet Firdusi (c. 930–1020). In his *Shahnameh*, or Book of Kings (vol. 7, section 39), an epic of ancient Iran completed in 1011, he reports, giving no exact date, that King Bahram Gur, wishing to make his people happy, asked his subjects what they wanted. The reply: 'We see that the whole world prospers, blessings arising everywhere, except that the poor complain of the king and their misfortune, for the rich drink wine to the sound of music, their heads crowned with flowers, while poor men like us, who drink without music or flowers, count for nothing.' The king at once dispatched a messenger to Shankal, the king of India, whose daughter he had married. 'O ever-helpful king,' he beseeched him, 'choose ten thousand Luri, men and women, expert in lute-playing!' When the Luri arrived, the king welcomed them and gave each one an ox, an ass, and some corn, to turn them into farmers. They, in return, were to play music for the poor for free. The Luri 'left, ate the oxen and the corn, and returned a year later, with sunken cheeks. The king told them: "You should not have wasted the seed, the corn, and the harvest. You still have your donkeys: load them up with your possessions, prepare your musical instruments, and put strings of silk upon them." And even today the Luri roam the world following the king's just words, seeking their livelihood, sharing dens with dogs and wolves, and thieving night and day as they go.'

It is interesting to complement this first document by some definitions given by a modern Persian dictionary [3]. The entry under Koli reads: 'Remnants of the tribe of Hindu musicians who came to Iran during the reign of Bahram Gur. They are nomads, found everywhere. Also called Luri and Luli.' Under the entry Luli: 'also means Luri and Koli; figuratively, a hand-some young man, carefree, a singer, reciter of poems, or musician'. We may fill out these definitions by remarking that the word Luli is common in poetry; it appears in nearly all Sufi poems. For the Sufis the Luli is the singer, musician, and reciter of poems; by looking upon his face listeners commune with abso-lute beauty, the divinity. In ancient and modern Persian there are many adjectives derived from the word *luli*, like *luli vash* (beautiful face), *luli sefate* (behaving like a Luli, characterized by instability). Moreover, the presence or long stay of Gypsies on

the Iranian plateau is confirmed by borrowings from Iranian languages: 'the vocabulary of all Gypsy dialects retains signs of this stay' [21, p. 17; see also 37].

The second document comes from the Arab historian Hamza of Isfahan, who in the year 940 recounted a similar story, using the word Zott instead of Luri, and giving the figure of twelve thousand. Mention of these Zott dates from the seventh century; some are said to have deserted from the Persian army and founded colonies on the coasts of Arabia and Persia [74].

It may perhaps be reasonable to suppose that there were large-scale migrations from India to Persia. But did the Gypsies leave before the year 1000? Some writers argue that there was a first major migration towards the twelfth century, at the time of Genghis Khan, and a second during the reign of Tamerlane in the fourteenth century. José Carlos de Luna objects that there were some migrations long before this, and that the Gypsies would remember the name of a ruler who had driven them out so recently [73]. The only plausible hypothesis is that the Gypsy migration, part of that ceaseless drift of nomadic tribes moving westwards from India, occurred in several waves, probably beginning in the ninth century.

If the Gypsies are originally from India, which part of the subcontinent do they come from, and to which cultural group do they belong? Here again there are many hypotheses. Grellmann said they were from north-west India, from the Sind region, but he went on to specify the kingdom of Guzrate, in the province of Tatta. That was also the view of Paulino de San Bartolomé, who knew India and its dialects intimately [48, 39]. Miklosich held that the Gypsy language was related to a group of languages in the Hindu Kush which had certain peculiarities that distinguished them from Indian languages proper. In 1915 Woolner pointed to evidence of a relationship with central India, and in 1927 Turner stressed the dual kinship of the Gypsy language. According to Jules Bloch, we might well imagine groups originally from Hindustan migrating to the borders of Iran, which would explain the various influences, and present-day Afghan territories may include some Gypsies [17, p. 25; see also 98, pp. 30–59 and 63]. Travellers' accounts, too, suggest comparisons with the inhabitants of those regions of India from

◁ Yugoslav Gypsy woman
with children, France

which we think the Gypsies came: there are striking similarities between the two groups [93; 26, p. 34].

Conclusions have also been drawn from anthropological data. But the studies undertaken so far have involved sample spaces too small to produce really useful and clear results, especially since the methods have been challenged [90, 38 and the critical analysis in 50, for example].

One other point remains: what routes did the Gypsies follow after they left India? Here again there is no lack of guesswork, and many critical researchers are baffled, even irritated, by Gypsy tales. Here, for instance, is Sebastian Münster questioning the 'Egyptians' in the sixteenth century:

> I myself have heard from a rascal of this fine band, who belonged to their count's council, that when they want to go back to their country, they are obliged to travel through a land inhabited by Pygmies, short men, a cubit high, who are caught in traps or nets, as hares are caught here. And when I asked him where this region was, he replied that it was far beyond the Holy Land, even beyond Babylon. I then said to him, so your Lower Egypt is not in Africa near the Nile, but in Asia near the River Ganges, or near the River Indus, which assertion he rejected with some further nonsense, namely that he knew not where was Africa, or Asia [82; see also 68, p. 17].

But these hypotheses about Gypsy dispersion, although still discussed in contemporary works, are necessarily circumscribed by the certainties that have since been unearthed from written records.

Some Certainties

Linguistics, which first provided vital clues, has now given us some certainties. The earliest glossaries by Borde and Vulcanius, though often inaccurate in details, could have been of considerable value. But the works of these two pioneers failed to make any real impact in the learned world. Not long after they wrote, a fog of massive persecution clouded all sensible inquiry. Borde and Vulcanius lived at a time when West Europeans still saw Gypsy immigrants as human beings, albeit foreigners. Later, when murderous prejudices took root, Borde's phrase-list dropped from sight, while Vulcanius's list was occasionally plagiarized, without any comprehension of its significance. It was only after the Enlightenment, and the beginning of what might be called modern scientific inquiry into the Gypsies, that Vulcanius and Borde were rediscovered, to the amazement of the learned world.

The real breakthrough came in the late eighteenth century, almost by chance: Stephan Vályi, a Hungarian student at the University of Leyden, came across three students from the Malabar coast (in south-west India). Noting the resemblance between their language and that of the Gypsies in his home town of Györ, he drew up a vocabulary with them, which he was later able to discuss at length with other Gypsies.

The likely origin of the Gypsies had been found. Linguists at once followed the trail, and works were soon published by Rüdiger and Grellmann in Germany and by Jacob Bryant in Britain. Examining the Gypsy language in Germany, Transylvania, and Hungary, Grellmann discovered a number of important words from India, with the same declensions and conjugations. A few years earlier, Rüdiger, referring to grammars published in Europe in the late eighteenth century, had settled on India as the land of Gypsy origin [48, 103]. Other works were published in the eighteenth century by Marsden, Richardson, Hervás y Panduro, Ludolf, and Hidalgo and in the nineteenth century by Baudrimont, Predari, Kalina, Borrow, Campuzano, Jiménez, Mayo, Cruzillo, Kogalniceanu, Ascoli, Paspati, Artout, Wlislocki, Miklosich and many others, including Pott, who was the first to attempt a rigorous demonstration of the Indian origin of the Gypsy language. The inventor of comparative phonetics and etymology for Indo-European languages, Pott took research a long step forward. He believed that the Gypsies came originally from northern India and that they had spoken a single language until their dispersion gave rise to different dialects [92].

The Gypsy language, *romani čib*, seems to be an Indian

language. Like the languages currently spoken in northern India—Hindi, Bengali, Punjabi, Gujerati, Rajasthani—it is descended from Sanskrit. Romany's closest relation is probably Hindi: 'this is not the sort of kinship that can be demonstrated only by learned linguistic laws and complicated deductions: it is obvious and palpable, for the relation is very close' [78, p. 12; see also 21, pp. 15–26]. Since the beginning of the twentieth century, research has been increasingly refined. The works of Sampson and Turner in Britain have been particularly valuable. Sampson established the similarity between the Rom Gypsies and the Indian Dom caste [106, 107, 108]. Many facts suggest their similarity and an origin in central India [see the discussion in 60]. Turner showed that the Gypsy language belonged to the central India group and had later borrowed from north-western India [120]. While the Rom-Dom analogy rests on well-founded observations, the supposed close relations between Rom and Banjara, or Rom and Jat, remain hypothetical [see for example 25 and 98].

Examination of the vocabulary and grammatical structures of Gypsy dialects in various countries has given us some idea of the paths taken during the dispersion. The further away from India, the more marked are the loss of basic vocabulary and the corresponding increase in the number of words borrowed from other languages. Locating the origin of borrowed words makes it possible to trace the routes. (See the table on page 00.) A similar method allows us to determine how long the Gypsies stayed in any particular country. In 1936 Martin Block wrote that 'the number of foreign words adopted by the Gypsies corresponds to the length of their sojourn in different countries' [18]. Miklosich's combination of the two methods reveals that some tribes stayed in Iran, Asia Minor and Greece (there are many words from medieval Greek), Armenia (*grast*: 'horse'; *bov*: 'pot'; *mortí*: 'skin'; *kotór*: 'morsel', 'piece'), and many other regions, including the Balkans, Hungary, Romania, and Germany. But beyond Central Europe the conclusions are less precise, because of the dispersion of the various groups, their retracing of some routes, and the criss-crossing of others. All this makes the map of migrations illegible. Nevertheless, crucial information has been gleaned from this research.

Lexical Comparisons Showing the Origin of the Gypsy Language and Borrowings Made during Migrations

[examples given by Georges Calvet in 21]

Gypsy (Kalderaš)	Hindi	Punjabi	
av-	ā-	āu	'to come'
de-	de-	de-	'to give'
dikh-	dekh-	dekh-	'to see'
ker-	kar-	kar-	'to do'
khel-	khel-	khel-	'to play'
phir-	phir-	phir-	'to walk'
čor	čor	čor	'thief'
kan	kān	kann	'ear'
nakh	nāk	nakk	'nose'
andré	andar	andar	'inside'
kaló	kālā	kālā	'black'
loló	lāl	lāl	'red'
jekh	ek	ikk	'one'
duj	do	do	'two'

Gypsy (Kalderaš)	Persian	Kurdish	
baxt	baxt	bext	'luck'
kež	kaž	kež	'raw silk'
koró	kūr	kor	'blind'
tang	tang	teng	'narrow'
zor	zūr	zor	'strength'

Gypsy (Kalderaš)	Greek	
drom	dromos	'road'
kakavi	kakkabê	'kettle'
kokalo	kokkalon	'bone'
stadi	skiadi	'hat'
xoli	kholê	'anger'
zumi	zoumi	'soup'

One of the classic studies investigated the Gypsy language in Wales [108; see also another classic: 47]. John Sampson discovered 150 roots of English origin there, as against 518 of Indian origin (more than half the root-words are still in use). A

37

total of 430 borrowed words were identified, of which about 40 were of Welsh origin, 90 of Greek, 60 of Slav, and a similar number of Iranian, the rest being of Romanian, German, French, and other origins. A recent count in a highly hetero-geneous Sinto dialect showed that 41 per cent of the words were of Indian origin [112; see also 77, 54, 22, 124].

The more recent dispersion is easier to follow, since there are unambiguous documents from the mid-fourteenth century on-wards. It has been noted that 'the prehistory of the Gypsies ends, and their history begins, at the beginning of the fourteenth century', [133, p. 17; see also 129, 131].

In 1322 two Franciscans on a pilgrimage to the Holy Land saw cave-dwelling Gypsies near Candia, in Crete. Some twenty-five years later, in 1348, 'Cingarije' were reported in Serbia (and had probably been there for half a century). At about the same time, a 'Gypsy fief' (*feudum Acinganorum*) was established on the island of Corfu. It lasted into the nineteenth century and its inhabi-tants, blacksmiths and cauldron-makers for the most part, were exempt from taxes and legally subject only to their 'baron', except as regards capital crimes. In 1378 many 'Cygans' are mentioned in judicial chronicles in Zagreb, and in the same year the Venetian governor of Nauplia, on the Peloponnesian coast, renewed the privileges enjoyed by the local 'Acingani'. At Modon, also in the Peloponnese, Gypsies were settled at the foot of Mount Gype. In 1399 the book of death sentences in a seigniory in Bohemia mentions a 'black Gypsy'. In 1370 some forty Gypsy families in Walachia were given as slaves to the monastery of Saint Anthony; the gift was repeated by Mircea I, *voïvode* (chief) of Walachia, in 1386. In the late fourteenth century the various groups seem to have settled down somewhat, but early in the fifteenth they began moving again [see 131].

With the fifteenth century we have more written documents. Moldavia and Hungary were the main centres of dispersion at the time. The Gypsies then moved north and north-west. Various chroniclers mention their presence in Germany be-tween 1407 and 1416. In 1416 the town of Kronshtadt, in Transylvania, made gifts of silver and victuals to 'the lord Emaus of Egypt and his 120 companions'. A year later Gypsies passed through the Hanseatic cities, and their presence is men-

Les Bohémiens, Lucas de Leyde, 1420

tioned in Saxony, Bavaria, Hesse, and near the Swiss frontier. They travelled in groups, including women and children, and were led by a 'chief', 'duke', 'count', 'captain', or 'voïvode'. They had horses and sometimes wagons for their baggage, and they always described themselves as penitents or pilgrims, living off private and public charity. In August 1418 they were in Zurich. A year later, 22 August 1419, a group arrived at Châtillon-en-Dombes (now called Châtillon-sur-Chalaronne) in the Ain, France. They were well received, for they carried letters from

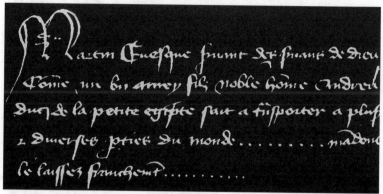

Translation of papal bull of Pope Martin V, 1423

the emperor and the duke of Savoy. They were given six florins
in gifts. Two days later they appeared at Mâcon, led by Duke
Andrew, and camped at Saint-Laurent, near the Saône. The
local people were very impressed by these newcomers, who 'lay
in the fields like beasts' [for Châtillon, see 81]. On 1 October
1419 a similar group pitched their tents near Sisteron, where
they remained for two days. In September 1421 a group settled
at Bruges, and in October a 'count of Little Egypt' brought his
troops to Arras. Again chroniclers record universal astonish-
ment, listing the group in the registers under the heading:
'Marvels. Arrivals of strangers from the land of Egypt' [129,
p. 19].

In July 1422 a group led by Duke Michael was refused
admittance to Basle; it joined with others and a larger troop,
commanded by Duke Andrew, set out for Italy. They arrived in
Bologna on 18 July, and left after two eventful weeks. (When the
Gypsies informed the Bolognese that the king of Hungary had
given them permission to steal at will during their seven-year
pilgrimage, the Bolognese responded by robbing the Gypsies.)
The band arrived at Forlì at the beginning of August, still
claiming to be *en route* to Rome. There are no written documents
of the rest of the journey, and no report of their arrival in Rome
or any visit to the Pope. But they soon turned up bearing letters
of recommendation from Pope Martin v, though whether
genuine or forged is not known. The effect was the same either
way, since papal bulls were always treated with respect, by

ecclesiastical and lay authorities alike. A copy of a translation of one of these bulls, dated 15 December 1423, has been discovered [130]. In it the Pope requests all church and civil authorities to let Duke Andrew circulate wherever he chooses, safely and freely, 'with his companions, servants, horses, baggage, goods and belongings . . . on horseback and on foot, by sea or land', without paying any tax or toll [130, pp. 13–19].

There is also a letter from Sigismund, emperor of Germany, from the same period (probably 1417), granting similar privileges to the Gypsies:

> We, Sigismund . . . king of Hungary, Bohemia, Dalmatia, Croatia, and other lands . . .
>
> Our faithful Ladislas, voïvode of the Gypsies, and others dependent on him have humbly beseeched Us to bear witness to our especial benevolence. It has pleased Us to receive their compliant request and not to refuse them this present letter. In consequence, should the aforesaid Ladislas and his people present themselves in any place, town or village, within Our Empire, We enjoin you to manifest your loyalty to us. You will protect them in every way, so that Voïvode Ladislas and his subjects the Gypsies can reside within your walls. Should there be found among them some drunken woman, should any troublesome incident, of whatever nature, occur, it is Our will and formal command that the said Voïvode Ladislas and he alone exercise the right to punish and absolve, to the exclusion of you all.

Between 1415 and 1430 groups of Gypsies spread throughout Western Europe. In 1425 a group led by 'Don Johan of Egipte Menor' is mentioned in the crown registers in Aragon as having a safe-conduct issued by King Alfonso v on 12 January 1425, in Zaragoza. The king informs all his vassals that 'our dear devoted Don Johan of Egipte Menor' is travelling with permission and should be 'well-treated and welcomed'. On pain of arousing royal anger and indignation, he must be allowed 'to go, stay and pass through' (*anar, star e passar*) at will, along 'with those accompanying him, his mounts, clothes, goods, gold . . .', all necessary protection being provided. This safe-conduct was valid for three months [5, 72].

In 1427 it was the turn of the city of Paris to be astounded by the appearance of Gypsies at its gates. The event is recorded in the *Journal d'un bourgeois de Paris*, and was described this way by a modern French author:

> The new arrivals claimed to have come from Rome, where they had seen the Pope, 'and had already been travelling for five years before their arrival in Paris' on 17 August 1427. The period—five years—is accurate, since they were recorded on the road to Rome in 1422. First there arrived in Paris 'twelve penitents, as they said: there were a duke, a count and ten men all on horseback' and later, 'on the day of the Beheading of Saint John, the common herd arrived, who were not allowed to enter Paris; but, by order of the court, they were accommodated in La-Chapelle-Saint-Denis. Men, women and children, they did not number more than 100 or 120 . . . ; the men were very dark and their hair was crisp; the women were the ugliest and swarthiest one could see; their faces were all lined and their hair was as black as a horse's tail . . . they were the poorest creatures ever seen coming in to France in living memory. In spite of their poverty there were among them witches who, looking at people's hands, revealed their past and foretold their future, and sowed discord in many households by telling the husband "your wife has made you cuckold", or the wife "your husband has deceived you". But the worst was that as their patter went on, either by magic, or otherwise, or with the help of the devil, or by their dexterity, they emptied into their own purses those of their listeners, so it was said. Truth to say, I went to speak to them three or four times and I never lost a farthing and I did not see them looking at hands. But people repeated it all over, and news of it reached the bishop of Paris. He went to see them, bringing with him a Franciscan named Petit Jacobin, who, on the bishop's order, preached a fine sermon, excommunicating all of both sexes who told fortunes, together with all those who had believed and shown

Fortune-telling, France ▷

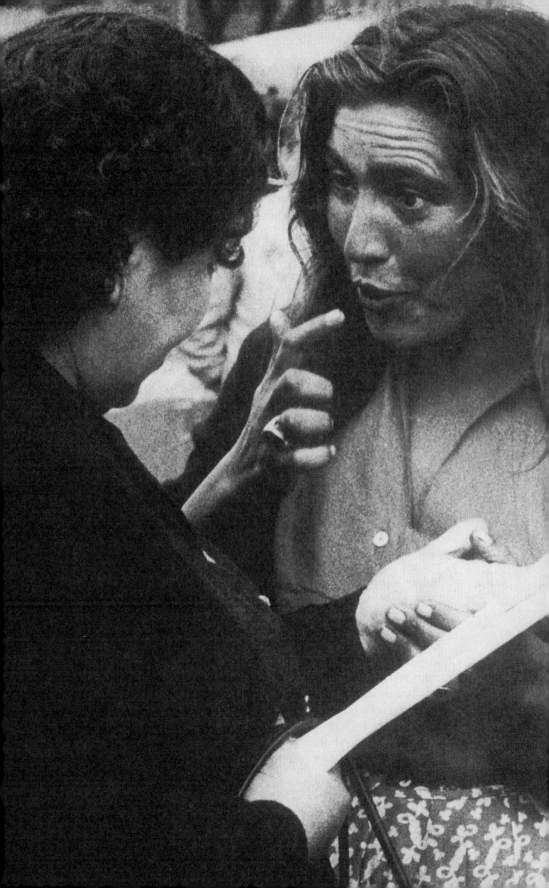

their hands; and they left on the day of Our Lady, in September, going towards Pontoise' [26, p. 55].

The wanderings continued. During the first quarter of the fifteenth century Gypsies roamed over much of Europe: Germany (1407), Switzerland (1418), France (1419), the Netherlands (1420), Italy (1422), Spain (1425), Poland (1428). Journeys to northern Europe began in the first half of the sixteenth century: Scotland (1505), Denmark (1505, coming from Scotland), Sweden (1512, coming from Denmark), England (the first evidence of a Gypsy presence dates from 1514, but there was probably an earlier immigration), Norway (1540, coming from England).

They entered Russia from the south in 1501, but seem to have reached Siberia only in 1721. Africa and the Americas had Gypsy immigration too, mainly as a result of the deportation of Gypsies from Portugal (mostly to Brazil) and Spain in the seventeenth century, and later from England and France. Finally, each wave of European emigration to the United States brought Gypsies with it [49, p. 17].

Every continent, perhaps even every country, has been affected by the Gypsy dispersion, by their many migrations, fast and slow, imperceptible and palpable, voluntary and forced. The groups that came to Western Europe sometimes settled down, but often continued to move from region to region and state to state. There were sweeping movements, as all Europe was explored, groups criss-crossing one another, trails becoming blurred. But the travels were gradually restricted by persecution; the scale of distances shrank, and became increasingly confined to the borders of single nations.

The first Gypsy wave thus left communities spread across Europe, settled in various places; many Gypsies had reduced the scope of their wandering, while some groups continued to move over greater distances. Sometimes Travellers of Indian origin encountered, and absorbed or were absorbed by, indigenous Travellers. In twelfth-century Scotland, for example, the name Tinkler or Tynker was given to a nomadic group with an identity and social organization of its own and a language that set it off from its environment. Cultural and social exchanges sometimes occurred between these Travellers and those of Indian origin, and this produced hybrid groups whose culture reflected their various origins (the English example is particularly significant in this respect). It is now often arbitrary—and sociologically, politically, anthropologically, and culturally irrelevant—to separate groups of Indian from those of indigenous origin (and sometimes even impossible to do so). They interact both locally (contacts between family groups, intermarriage) and more widely (in international Gypsy political organizations), and they occupy identical positions in an environment that treats all of them the same.

That first wave of groups from India was followed by another, several centuries later: it came in the second half of the nineteenth century, when the Gypsies in Romania were freed from slavery and emigrated throughout Europe, some going as far as the Americas. Apart from these two major waves of emigration, there have been other trickles. In the 1960s groups leaving Yugoslavia headed towards most states of Western Europe. Other significant migrations occurred too: in the 1960s, for example, many Travellers from Ireland crossed over to England and Wales; a few years later Ciganos from Portugal crossed into Spain, for economic reasons [on the reasons for migrations, see 71].

The arrival of different groups of immigrant Gypsies in each country at different times, the settlement and consequent reduction in the scope of the wandering of some, the regional or international movement of others, and the encounter with other indigenous nomads or subsequent arrivals have combined to produce both stratification and great cultural and linguistic diversity. The result is a multifarious Gypsy presence in each European state.

Statistics about the number of Gypsies are uncertain. The various official figures differ even in order of magnitude, since the criteria used (who is a Gypsy?) are always politically determined (and often vague). Some countries minimize the number of Gypsies or even deny their existence (so as to facilitate a policy of assimilation and deny cultural problems). Others inflate the numbers in an effort to exaggerate the alleged difficulties caused by Gypsies as an excuse for keeping them out. Moreover,

Gypsy encampment, Rumania

most Gypsies will not declare themselves as such in a census, partly because centuries of persecution have encouraged them to be cautious and partly because the word 'Gypsy' is meaningless in Gypsy culture itself. Statistical studies therefore provide no more than an illusion of accuracy, and comparative studies of different countries or periods are generally worthless.

The total world population of Gypsies may be in the order of 12 to 15 million. (But there are great uncertainties: by what criteria do we define 'Gypsy'? Are there Gypsies in India and Pakistan, and if so, how many?)

Gypsies have been called by many different names, and the people using them have had very different realities in mind. The names may arise from biased and short-sighted views of Gypsy history (as in France, where Gypsies were called Bohemians when they arrived bearing letters from the king of

Bohemia, or in Spain, where they were called Hungaros), from legends or myths (as with all the terms derived from 'Egypt': Gitans, Gitanos, Gypsies, and so on), from the distortion of some term used in the Gypsy language (like Manouches [Manuš] and Romanichals in France), or from more or less pejorative regional terms (Caraques and Boumians in the south of France, Camps-volants in Burgundy, Cascarots and Rabouins elsewhere), sometimes linked to perceptions of physical appearance (like Mustalainen or 'blacks', in Finland).

A rough estimate of the total number of Gypsies in Europe (excluding Turkey), east and west, would be as follows:

Albania:	20,000
Austria:	8,000 to 10,000
Belgium:	10,000 to 15,000
Bulgaria:	300,000 to 500,000
Cyprus:	500 to 1,000
Czechoslovakia:	300,000 to 400,000
Denmark:	1,000 to 2,000
Finland:	5,000 to 7,000
France:	220,000 to 300,000
West Germany:	55,000 to 65,000
Greece:	80,000 to 120,000
Hungary:	400,000 to 600,000
Ireland:	20,000 to 25,000
Italy:	60,000 to 90,000
Netherlands:	30,000 to 35,000
Norway:	250 to 500
Poland:	40,000
Portugal:	20,000 to 30,000
Romania:	500,000 to 800,000
Spain:	300,000 to 450,000
Sweden:	60,000 to 100,000
Switzerland:	12,000 to 15,000
United Kingdom:	80,000 to 110,000
USSR:	200,000 to 300,000
Yugoslavia:	700,000 to 900,000
TOTAL:	3,421,750 to 4,935,500

2

GYPSY SOCIETY

An exhaustive study of the culture of all Gypsy populations would take a whole collection of volumes. Of course, every population is complex, and any synthesis is necessarily over-simplified, but in this case it might well be unusually misleading: one can really talk about only *one* particular Gypsy group, and any generalization on that basis would be a distortion. 'The really absurd thing, caused by a simple semantic misunder-standing, has been the long search for the "true Gypsy", perhaps the most futile dispute in the entire history of Gypsy studies' [89, p. 45].

The latest works show that overly general approaches have fallen short of accuracy when dealing with such a complex, multi-faceted reality. Recent detailed studies of Gypsy societies [especially 89, 140] have done much to change our thinking; but these are by authors who have worked for several years with particular, small, limited Gypsy groups. Studies of other groups would produce different conclusions. Since the subject is complex and space is limited, I have tried to cut out all inessentials in order to concentrate on the basic considerations that help us to understand the dynamics of a culture and life-style. To do this, I have relied on some of the latest ethnographic works; in addition, the information contained in a recent report for the Council of Europe [71, part 1] complements many of the observations made in the original French edition of this book.

The world's Gypsy populations form a mosaic of small diverse groups. Two essential considerations follow. First, a mosaic is a whole whose component features are linked to one another. The whole is structured by these links that run through it. The Gypsy

◁ Chest containing religious
  relics at site of pilgrimage, France

populations can be considered as forming an organized whole, even though its structure is not rigid, but ever-changing. Over and above the variety, a meaningful configuration still remains.

Second, each component of the whole has its own special features, which make it appear, when viewed in isolation, quite different from every other component of the mosaic: its texture is special, and its substance may be too. No description of the organization of the whole can give a proper account of each of the parts, and the analysis of any particular part cannot be generalized to the whole. At the same time, the parts, while essential to the composition of the whole, acquire their importance and their *raison d'être* only in the framework of the whole that holds them together.

I will try to analyse the role and place of those features that separate the various Gypsy groups and those that bring them together. Differences and similarities are complementary rather than antagonistic, and the two aspects combine to mark out the position of the group in society: it is through the interplay of the distinctive contrasts that each group acquires its own identity.

Nomadism

Not all Gypsies are nomads, and not all nomads are Gypsies. Nomadism is an important feature of Gypsy being, but not in the usual dictionary sense of nomads as people who are continually on the move from place to place.

The mistaken idea that Gypsy is synonymous with wanderer arose partly from the influx into Western Europe and the Americas, especially in the late nineteenth century and even as late as the 1950s, of large-scale Gypsy migrations from the east, in particular Gypsies freed from slavery in the Romanian principalities. Some of them, after stays in Poland, Hungary, or Russia, left for Western Europe and the Americas, where they continued travelling, but mainly on a smaller scale. These large recent migrations merged with the communities that had been criss-crossing all Europe since the fifteenth or sixteenth century, on foot, on horseback, in wagons and finally in caravans. Even though they tended to settle briefly whenever they were allowed to, the idea that Gypsies are atavistically mobile gained ground. Then there is the example of the 'great Gypsy travellers', the people who, despite the difficulties of moving around and camping in the late twentieth century, traverse whole regions and nations. The passage of their caravans, their constant motion with what an outsider sees as no apparent reason, fuel the fiction of the nomad who is alien everywhere, never 'belonging', ever moving on.

If we take geographical movement alone, Gypsy populations present a whole spectrum of situations, from the family that roams across Europe in long wide caravans drawn by the most powerful cars to the family mired in a shanty town with no hope of ever getting out. Some stop for the winter and move on in the spring, living lives of two seasons, one for travelling, one for stopping. Some stay in the same spot for several years before moving on to a new town, nation or continent, pulling up stakes ten or fifteen times in their lives. Some leave a place hoping to settle elsewhere but come back, disappointed by living conditions in the new area, or ill-received by the Gypsies already living there, or reluctant to mix with them. Some leave for a few weeks or months, either at regular intervals or occasionally, then return to their place of departure. Some move about in nomadic occupations: groups of coppersmiths and tinkers, hawkers and showmen have regular customers or areas, and nomadism then becomes regular, itineraries fixed. Hundreds or thousands of Gypsies move for the great meetings, the pilgrimages, the fairs. On occasions like these, many 'sedentaries' temporarily take to the road again. There are itinerant basket-makers who, while constantly nomadic, never overstep the boundaries of a French *département* or a few cantons. There are horse-traders who ride their mules from fair to fair throughout the year, sleeping under the bridges of Andalusian streams run dry. There are peddlers of high-priced oriental carpets or ivory who stay in the luxury hotels of capital cities.

Then there is the variety of means of transport, ranging from the fastest to the slowest, from the aeroplane to the horse-drawn caravan, from the most sophisticated to the most rickety, from the CB-equipped American van to the wagon rolling along on grinding axles. And this variety exists within a single country,

51

Travellers' caravan ▷

and among people living side by side, sometimes in the very same stopping place. But whether in a tent, a mud hut, a caravan or a house, in a grotto or hotel or lorry without wheels, on a carpet or in the mud, it is the *style* that is Gypsy [see 139, p. 34]. The Gypsy who has come to rest sees a house as a huge tent: the one large room, essential feature of community life, and the furnishings, decoration, and arrangement of objects are all in that certain style. The halt, whether long or short, voluntary or not, is always seen as temporary, except by families who have finally lost hope of leaving and therefore any reason for living. As Jean Cocteau wrote of the famous Gypsy guitarist Django Reinhardt, 'He lived as one dreams of living, in a caravan. And even when it was no longer a caravan, somehow it still was' [quoted by 40]. Just as settled people remain settled people even when they travel, so the Gypsy is a nomad even when not travelling. A Gypsy at rest remains a traveller. So it is really more accurate to speak of *sedentarized* Gypsies rather than *sedentary* Gypsies, for the former suggests a temporary condition for people who still consider movement meaningful and vital. Nomadism is a state of mind more than a state of fact. Its existence and importance are psychological more than geographical [cf. 69, p. 42].

Nomadism fulfils several functions for the Gypsies. It is part of their identity, it makes for adaptability and flexibility, and it facilitates social cohesion—three inseparable features of this life-style. As an element of identity, being 'Travellers' lets the Gypsies mark themselves off from those who aren't, the gadže, the non-Gypsies, the peasants, the sedentary, rigid, and rooted. Travel is a symbol and an honour: the sentence 'We are Travellers' is a necessary and sufficient statement of identity for those who say it. It explains everything. Travellers move on. Their living space is experience itself, never a shut or bounded territory, but a flexible identity unattached to any particular piece of earth: the land of the Gypsies lies within themselves.

Just as the crossing of spaces has little to do with the unfolding of history, so the notion of a boundless, undivided space casts the duration of the journey, and of existence itself, into an infinite, continuous time-scale. Places are not links but only stages. The present contains both the past gone by and the future, which will be here soon enough—it need not be imagined. The present is so important that you can both forget and not bother to look ahead, leave things behind by shifting the problems created by others, bend to arbitrary obligations without breaking [cf. 70]. This notion of time and space provides a flexibility and adaptability that have enabled Gypsy populations to live for centuries scattered among hostile peoples, meanwhile developing the features of a special culture of their own.

Nomadism, movement, and the fact of being Travellers have always been essential in the formation and maintenance of this culture. Settling down probably would have meant borrowing more from surrounding populations, and more marriages with others. But this assumption should not be pushed too far: the situation of Gypsies has not permitted such exchanges, and

Shrine in lorry of Kalderaš, France

neither the more than five centuries of slavery in the Romanian principalities nor the equally lengthy attempts at assimilation in Spain have blunted the adaptive capacities of a culture forged at the fringes of society. The Kalé of Spain still consider themselves Kalé, and the descendants of slaves scattered across the world are often regarded as the most 'traditional' Gypsies. But even more important, if the Travellers had settled down, there would have been a break-up of scattered social groups, and they would no longer have been bound together by travelling. Nomadism enables different groups to live side by side for a while, and individuals from the same group but different places to meet and marry. The relations of contrast or similarity thus formed, depending on whether the encounters involve different or similar people, help to organize society, to arouse comparison and homogeneity, and to forge consensus by mutual respect for shared values.

Since the second world war, however, travel has become difficult, both for economic reasons and because of the plethora of rules and regulations. The industrialization of all Western lands has plugged the holes through which nomads pass and overhauled their opportunities for economic adaptation. Urbanization makes it more difficult to set up camps and provides more excuses for eviction—increasingly common since nomadism, real or imagined, is a feature of Gypsy life that non-Gypsies find worrying and upsetting [70]. The territorialization of the nomad spells crisis, both for the society that refuses to accept the Traveller, and for Gypsy society, which is now splitting to produce two cultures: one, geographically constant and above all homogeneous, is characteristic of Gypsies who are nomadic, or at least potentially nomadic, since they are sedentarized only temporarily and voluntarily; the other, geographically diffuse and tending to become heterogeneous, is disintegrating into separate fragments, characteristic of those who have been forced to settle and are becoming sedentary. The quality of travel is being transformed too, since it is easier to get from place to place rapidly but harder and harder to stay anywhere. Travel is becoming mere journey, and exchanges (especially economic ones) with the surrounding environment at the many stop-overs are fast disappearing. For many Gypsies the road is becoming a tunnel. But nomadism is still a state of mind, and Gypsy social organization constantly draws individuals and their groups away from fixed places.

Social Structures

From the Gypsy point of view, there is no such group as Gypsies. Their vocabulary has no word to designate themselves as a whole. They are defined as such by the views and attitudes of others, and it is their relations with others that set the limits of the whole [cf. 69, p. 72]. But although the members of so-called Gypsy society find it hard to think of themselves in terms of the totality they are supposed to form, this does not mean that they constitute an unformed mass, each element of which has nothing in common with the others. Conversely, the whole is not monolithic, each component having everything, or nearly everything, in common with the others.

Variety is institutionalized. The so-called Gypsies live their culture through a system of distinctive contrasts. Everyone sees society through the particular viewpoint of the social group to which he or she belongs. So there can be as many conceptions and definitions of 'Gypsy' as there are different parts within the 'Gypsy' whole. To start with, then, let us look at the functions of names: what does each part of the so-called Gypsy whole call itself, and what does it call others? [This approach has been followed, and its necessity demonstrated, by 140: see chapter 2, pp. 74–105; and by 89.]

> Well, it won't be easy, but I'll try. I think I understand what you want to know: 'How can you tell if someone is a Gitan?' Is that all? It's a big question. I have to think about it. There are shadings . . . The difference between the Sinti and the other Gypsies, for example, is like the difference between a Frenchman and a European. About like that. Or between a peasant and a guy from the town: it's all a matter of families. There's a difference between the ones close to you, the ones you love, and the ones you don't. For Travel-

lers—a Manuš, for example—it's family ties that count. Either he loves one side or he doesn't, and it's sort of just the same overall. But as for gadže, the difference is that there are so many, the world's full of them. That doesn't mean that we don't make distinctions among ourselves, internally. But as far as the gadže go, we all agree.

The ones who have stayed closest to tradition are the 'Hungarians', the Tsiganes, or whatever you want to call them. They have clans, more closed than we Sinti. There are some almost everywhere now, and when people say 'Gypsy', they're talking about the whole. We say Traveller because we prefer it, we want to mark ourselves off, because we can't say 'Hungarian' since we're not, and we don't like to be called 'Bohemians'. Sinti is all right too! [89]

So many terms appear here in just a few sentences: Gitan, Sinti, Traveller, Manuš, gadže, Hungarian, Bohemian, Gypsies. The speaker locates them relative to one another. Further questioning locates these terms more precisely: 'For a Frenchman, there are Frenchmen, English, Chinese, Italians, and so on. For us, there are us and the gadže. There's the difference! . . . My world is my own family; it's as if the others, the jerks as we call them, didn't exist.' The irreducible distinction between 'us' and 'my world', and the others, the 'non-existent' others, the gadže, the 'jerks', is obvious. Gypsies of the Rom group in the United States, for example, use the term Bojaš to apply both to all Gypsies of other groups and to 'Travellers' of Irish or Scottish origin.

'Bojaš' may also apply to people from the group who call themselves 'Ludar', made up of 'Romanians'. The Rom themselves call 'Hungarian' Gypsies (who are professional musicians) Bašalde, which literally means 'noise-makers' [104].

In this segmented social universe, there is no structure of chieftancy. The 'king of the Gypsies' is a figment of the imagination of the gadže, and neither the Roma as a whole nor any of the sub-groups have a formal leader.

Historical evidence indicates that when they first appeared in France in the fifteenth century, the Gypsies were led by men

Zanko, leader of a Kalderaš group, France

calling themselves 'count' or 'duke' of Little Egypt; from the
sixteenth to eighteenth centuries, we find mention of 'captains',
often aided by 'lieutenants'. In Hungary and Poland the titles
voïvode, *vajda*, *vataf*, and *wojt* were used. We also find *bulibasha* in
the Danube principalities, *ataman* in the Ukraine, and 'lord' in
Scotland. All these terms are obviously borrowed, and were
sometimes used, especially in Poland, to give a title to one Gypsy
designated by kings or lords to govern other Gypsies working on
their lands. These terms therefore do not reflect a social hier-
archy, but were an instance of superficial adaptation to local
conditions and customs.

The very notion of chief seems not to exist, although some
individuals do acquire positions of special influence and *de facto*
leadership at the level of the family community. These family
leaders are not necessarily elders. Old people enjoy esteem if
they deserve it, and terms of respect are then used. But Gypsy
society is not a gerontocracy, and an old man whose only notable

59

Gypsy tribunal (*kris*), France ▷

Keeping history alive

quality is his age is not considered a leader. To be a leader requires respect, which is earned mainly by being 'well-thought-of'.

If every man is a potential leader of his family group, what are the qualifications for this role? Certain qualities are usually necessary but never sufficient: an age that allows a man to have a large family; some degree of wealth, which depends both on family position and on a combination of luck and skill in work and in business; an ability to speak effectively so as to stand out in meetings. But these alone are not enough: a rich man with a large family will not be well-thought-of if he is considered stupid, even if he is a good speaker; on the other hand, if a man who is well-thought-of runs into economic problems, that will not necessarily diminish his prestige. Two criteria that seem, on the contrary, to be necessary and usually sufficient are intelligence and showing of respect for others. In the Gypsy view, both these qualities are summed up in intelligence, since the intelligent man will be discreet, will not claim to be superior to others, will respect others, and will prosper. An alternative and roughly equivalent summary would be this: to be well thought of. In that case, the reverse chain of reasoning operates: an individual is well-thought-of because he is worthy of being so regarded by others, because he is intelligent, respectful of others, and has a large family that is itself well-thought-of (an individual cannot be well-thought-of unless his family is too). Thus the entire structure of thought rests on a few basic values.

The role of family leader is a collective creation. A prospective leader must not put himself forward but must be brought to his position by others. Any man who called himself 'chief' or tried to act as a leader without prior consensus would by definition no longer be worthy of leadership. It would be a social gaffe, and if a man is to have any chance of earning respect, he must not make such errors. He must always have behaved 'wisely' and be prudent in his actions and stands, especially in formal gatherings. Finally, not even the leader of an extended family could conceivably call himself or be considered the representative of a group, however small. Such situations come about only in special circumstances that facilitate dealings with the gadže, and the leader actually represents no more than his family group.

There is another subdivision in Rom Gypsy social organization, one not based on grounds of kinship: the *kumpanja*. This is a group formed by a temporary community at a campsite (of whatever sort), on the road, or at a place of work, the three not being necessarily linked. A kumpanja may be composed of one or more small family groups, or an extended family community, or a part of an extended family community, or even parts of several extended families. Several fragmented family communities may thus be involved in a single kumpanja. This is a temporary grouping constituted for practical reasons. A gathering of unrelated families of this type makes for flexible and adaptable organization: should the need arise, the kumpanja can be divided into smaller groups. It is also important in developing ties of mutual aid and solidarity between families, in redistributing earnings, and in making effective use of complementary skills.

When intermarriage occurs between families in the same kumpanja, each family must find some common relation with one or several of the others. It is then common to find canvassing and manipulation of genealogies, as people hunt back through their parents and grandparents to see whether one of their relatives or ancestors might have belonged to the same family as the people with whom a new tie is sought, or at least to a family somehow connected with them. If it appears that there have been no alliances on either the paternal or the maternal side, the past may be manipulated to provide justification for the present situation. In Gypsy consciousness, it is the present that counts.

The kumpanja plays another important role as well. Travelling divides family communities, and the kumpanja brings together those who are not kin. Or, to put it slightly differently: travelling separates relatives, while the kumpanja relates the unrelated. It thus introduces an element of unity.

The diversity of Gypsy society does not mean that there is no organization of the whole. The various groups maintain relations with one another, essentially through kinship ties, the social exchanges that occur at marriages, and the judicial regulation of tensions and conflicts between different groups.

Individuals are neither known nor recognized as such, but are always defined by the kinship group that affords them identity. When individuals meet, they seek to locate each other within a network of social relations. They are therefore never isolated or alone, but are always dependent on and in solidarity with the group in which they are included [69, pp. 45 and 61].

It could be argued that the collective, like the individual, is defined by the relations it maintains with others. But whereas the individual is fully immersed in the group and is its reflection and most faithful representative, the group seeks to mark itself off from others as sharply as possible. Virtually all actions are judged by collective criteria, and the individual is only the emanation of the group. Responsibility for individual actions is collective. If someone does something wrong, the close relatives

Reunion feast (*pačiv*), Spain

will be held responsible, and they will feel responsible too. If someone performs a worthy action, these same close relatives will derive the social benefits; so will the individual, of course, but only as a member of the group [69, pp. 73–89]. When individuals are joined in marriage, it is as the result of an agreement between the groups to which they belong [69, p. 53].

Relations between individuals are therefore relations between groups. When two people meet, they will identify themselves as members of a family and each will identify the other on the basis of family. What counts most of all in Gypsy social organization— more than individuals, more than the various ethnic sub-groups, and more even than the fragmentary family group—is the *system of family groups*, which exist in a never-ending dynamic of co-operation and struggle for influence. It is in the framework of this system that balances of power are established, and it is through this system that decisions are made.

Marriage, the Family, and Social Control

The term 'marriage' does not necessarily imply legal marriage, for Gypsies will often live together without getting sanction from the state. But contrary to the stereotype of the free-roaming Gypsy changing partners with abandon, marriages are serious events in Gypsy society, for they create alliances between families. Marriage links or the lack of them are thus of the greatest importance politically, since they balance relations between family groups. Among some Gypsies, arranged marriages are the rule; the community unites two families by endorsing the union of two of their members. Among others, in complete contrast, marriage usually occurs by elopement, but is equally important.

But marital unions are rarely completely free. For a family that wishes to maintain its cohesion, the ideal is to encourage marriage among relatives. On the other hand, the incest taboo and exogamy oblige people to marry at further remove. Unions thus create bonds, or strengthen existing ones, forcing people to co-operate and creating a minimum of social cohesion.

Marriage is most common within the extended kinship group. But were that an absolute rule, each community would turn into a micro-society that would soon become isolated from the others, and hence more vulnerable. So marriages are also common outside the family community, but not too far outside. Whereas kinship cements social co-operation and mutual aid, marriages outside the kinship group create affinities where there is no consanguinity. They thus weave a far-ranging network of social relations.

The procedures leading up to marriage are quite varied. In some groups, the actual union is the result of protracted negotiations between families. In others, the young people elope and then come to seek the pardon and agreement of their families. Sometimes, the elopement occurs after a more or less tacit agreement between the families. In any case, the act of marriage engages the whole community, since the relationship will link two family groups. Marriage is a collective phenomenon, a social compact between the parties. Because of intermarriage between extended family groups, the boundaries between

67

groups become permeable and flexible even though they are often supposed to be watertight and rigid: they undergo change even though they are widely perceived as eternal.

The terminology of kinship is very rich, and the density of kinship terms forms a tight mesh that quickly situates the individual [see 87, 88, 89, 114]. Unions create new mutual obligations for the individuals who enter into them and for the families. The boy passes from childhood to adulthood, with the right and duty to participate fully in social life. The girl becomes a woman, with an essential role as guarantor of order, cleanliness, and purity. Correlatively, she is the repository of the power to pollute, a power of particular importance, since the notion of impurity is central in social life and a feature of regulation and social control [on the role of women, see 4, 49, 85, 111, 114].

It is the birth of the first child, rather than the marriage, that lays the foundation for a stable family. Children are brought up collectively, since the family space is identical to the community space. Gypsy children, unrestrained by the supervision of a nuclear family, generally grow up in a wider arena that allows considerable initiative and experience, but with great physical and psychological security, for the community is on hand to watch and to help if necessary. Direct coercion in the form of corporal punishment is rare: for children, as for adults, the community's opinion is the ultimate arbiter. The community supervises the upbringing of children just as it cares for the elderly. The child is a full member of the group, and the consequent social cohesion provides security: the individual can never be alone and is never isolated.

Sexual relationships outside marriage are forbidden, particularly to women. They are viewed with particular distaste when they involve partners closely related by blood or marriage (father- and daughter-in-law, or sister- and brother-in-law), for such relations are synonymous with impurity, as are any sexual encounters with those who are supremely impure: the gadže.

Ideas about masculine and feminine roles are now changing. The influence of television, social workers, and the school system (which brings Gypsy children into contact with non-Gypsies and creates adolescence by delaying marriage) is altering role models. Moreover, the number of separations after

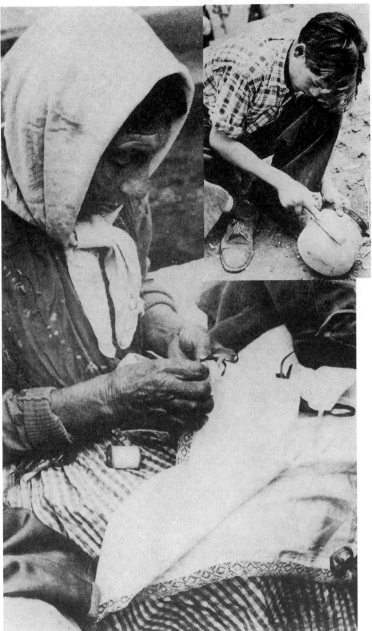

Sewing a wedding cloth. *Inset:* Making an earthenware pot, to be broken over the groom's head at the wedding ceremony

Rom wedding, Paris ▷

Breaking the pot — the more fragments the better!

Carrying the newly-weds

Wedding celebrations

Wedding celebrations

arranged marriages is on the rise and new rules are being introduced to adapt to this situation. In general, the young want more say in determining their own marriages.

If marriages create structures, measures of social control guarantee their consistency and survival. Social control operates diffusely, and is particularly effective because the community counts for more than the individual. A body of rules and taboos covers everything from the preparation of food and bodily cleanliness to dress and how to behave with members of the opposite sex.

Most of these rules and taboos are based on a dichotomy between 'pure' and 'impure' persons and things, between behaviour that maintains a state of purity and behaviour that soils and makes impure. This code is the basis on which sub-groups draw distinctions between themselves. Each group points to aspects of the behaviour of others that amount to impurity, and steps must therefore be taken to preserve a separation so as not to be polluted. As for the gadže, many of their actions are taboo for Gypsies and Travellers. Any interchange with them therefore entails the risk of pollution.

When taboos are violated and rules broken, there are procedures of reparation or justice. Offences must be made good to guarantee social order. If antagonisms develop between different families, some groups organize a community decision. In other groups a feud may result. The forms of discussion and reparation may also vary: an arrangement may be made between two partners; a handful of men may act as arbiters or mediators; a court of justice or tribunal may be convened. The essential thing is that society be regulated with the greatest possible consensus.

Sanctions are of various kinds. The guilty party will often have to pay a fine. Since responsibility is collective, a group of relatives will usually raise the amount to be paid. Supernatural sanctions, a last resort, carry great deterrent power: anyone who swears an oath and then commits perjury fears a terrible punishment. There is one sanction of extreme severity: an individual can be declared unclean and expelled from the community. This is the harshest punishment possible, for expulsion is a social and psychological death sentence.

In recent years Gypsies have faced new problems. The policy of rejection traditionally followed by state powers (described in the next chapter) caused the Gypsy communities to turn in on themselves. Organization of the internal life of isolated communities was the order of the day. More recently, government policies of assimilation and the influences on which they rest have undermined the cohesion of Gypsy society, obliging it increasingly to accommodate to a changing environment. The changing mores of the young generations and the effects of new state policies are beginning to make themselves felt.

Work

Gypsies work because they have to. Labour is not considered an end in itself but a means of maintaining independence, mobility, and adaptability. The Gypsies practise innumerable trades: tinning and metalworking (doing repairs, cleaning copper, gilding church objects, and so on), basket-making, caning or stuffing chairs, regrinding, sweeping chimneys, circus trades, music and dance, second-hand cars, vine-cutting and grape harvesting, gathering medicinal and various other herbs, fortune-telling.

These myriad occupations are, of course, adapted to place and time. In the United States, for example, many Gypsies tar roofs and driveways; in Eastern Europe, woodcraft remains important. Fortune-telling, practised in many countries, takes different forms depending on local customs and regulations: it is very common in the United States, where it is often based in commercial premises, with shop-fronts officially classified as tearooms or religious or occult bookshops. Before the spread of automatic photo machines, fortune-tellers often used photographic studios, the readings being described as an 'extra'. In some countries there are a few Gypsy doctors, lawyers, writers, and so on. The president of the Romanian Academy of Sciences in the 1970s was a Rom: Moron Niculescu, a professor of mathematics. Ion Voicu, the director of the Romanian National Philharmonic Orchestra, is also a Rom.

Traditionally, Gypsies and Travellers provide services to customers who are not Gypsies or Travellers. There is a sharp contrast between the co-operation and mutual aid that prevail within Gypsy groups, and the relations of exploitation they maintain with the gadže. Exploitation of one Gypsy by another is considered shameful and results in a loss of prestige all around; exploitation of the gadžo, however, wins esteem when it succeeds. A gadžo encountered by Gypsies, whatever the circumstances, is always a potential customer in some transaction, in the purchase or sale of some object or service. Economic life thus depends on seeking out the customer: the canvassing, prospecting, discussing, and haggling that might lead to a transaction is the main thing. A Gypsy going to work will say, *Žav te kerav butsi* (I'm going to do some work), but also *Phirav and o gav* (I'm walking in the town), *Phirav aj kerav* (I walk and do) or *Žav te mangav* (I'm going to ask) [40, p. 54; 140, p. 158].

Since all the Gypsies' income-producing activities involve the gadže, it might seem that Gypsies are dependent on those around them. In fact, however, here as in other respects Gypsies have considerable control of their environment: they know how to create and increase their '*gadžikano* capital', which ultimately rests on all their interchanges, and especially their 'good relations' with the people they live among [89 deals thoroughly with this important point, pp. 80, 144 ff.].

To maintain their mobility, Gypsies avoid trades that would tie them up before or after the specific transaction. They rarely take fixed employment, since their frequent and often unplanned moves require occupations that can be carried on quickly and in different places. They also have to avoid carrying heavy stock or equipment that cannot easily be moved. If there is a big job to be done, Gypsy workers may get together and hire equipment (a lorry, for example) or subcontract to a gadžo firm. Seasonal work like picking fruit, flowers, or vegetables is considered ideal both by Gypsies and their employers, who value labour mobility. In some countries it may be possible to spend most of the year harvesting some crop or other. Contracted jobs, quick and well paid, are highly sought after and enable Gypsies to organize both by family and in associations of workers. Maintenance work in harbours is one example, demolition work is another [20].

Repairing pans

Scrap-metal dealer, France

Independence and mobility require adaptability. It is rare for a Gypsy to have only one trade. They have to adapt to regulations that constantly change over time and vary from country to country. They must also deal with police practices that differ from place to place. A Gypsy might deal in scrap metal for several winter months in one place, for instance, and switch to door-to-door peddling in the spring, when he takes to the road again.

In the United States in particular, some Gypsies have also devised strategies to derive maximum benefit from the welfare system without falling into a situation of dependency. Their contact with the social services is sometimes similar to other economic contacts with their environment. According to one American author, 'They do not consider themselves a depressed minority having to beg for charity from the middle-class majority. On the contrary, welfare is to them an incredible stroke of luck, yet further proof of the gullibility of the gadže' [14, p. 78, see also p. 288]. On the other hand, there are also some genuinely destitute Gypsies: widows with young families, the disabled, those who have suffered a fire or other disaster, the old, the occasional person who is mentally ill. These people, who need and are fully entitled to state aid, often encounter suspicion, discrimination, and even outright rejection by the social security system. This is one reason why many Gypsies refuse to have anything to do with the institutions of the welfare state.

Economic relations within any given Gypsy group are governed by the principles of association and solidarity. Associations are formed on a basis of equality and profits are shared. Only in exceptional circumstances will one Gypsy employ another. Labour is an independent activity. The nobility of association is contrasted with the dependence of wage-labour; while it is considered an honour to be invited to be a partner in some job, to be employed would be seen as shameful. Association redistributes income, enables people to work in groups rather than alone, reinforces social cohesion, bolsters the tradition of group existence, and enables complementary skills to be pooled.

Apart from formal associations, there are also jobs done by all or part of the family (especially in agriculture). The activities of men and women tend to be complementary. When women

82

◁ Basket-weaver, Greece

work, their incomes are usually more regular than the men's, and are generally spent on everyday needs. Men's incomes, higher but less reliable, are used for big purchases and more conspicuous consumption (car, holiday meals, paying debts). There is often a sexual division of labour in relations with non-Gypsies. Among Rom in the United States, for example, it is women who deal with social workers and secure welfare payments, whereas the men generally handle contact with the local authorities and the police [see 49, 105, 114, 115].

Gypsies attach great importance to their social life, whereas work is a mere appendage of their personality, a necessary evil in a subsistence economy. In that sense it can be said that the Gypsy 'plays the boiler-maker', or 'plays the carpet-seller', or 'plays the fortune-teller' without really getting involved. What counts is for a Gypsy to live a life that is possible only because the multitude of petty dependencies on the gadže customers results in a kind of independence. Taking up a gadžo trade would be inconceivable, especially since working like a gadžo is polluting. Even in the face of great obstacles, Gypsies try to continue to work in the Gypsy way.

Conditions are fast growing worse, however. Factors such as increased urbanization, and the constraints of regulations which hamper and eliminate petty trades are narrowing the sources of income. Economic competition among Gypsies generates conflict and breaks bonds of solidarity. The flexibility that was once the strength of the system is becoming illusory, and is turning into a rigidity upheld by those who insist on defending tradition against changes they find intolerable. On the other hand, the Gypsy style of working, which regards free time as infinitely more important than income, has much in common with a trend now on the rise in Western societies. And Gypsies and Travellers are still generally able to adapt their economic activities to changes in their environment.

The Gypsy Way

Gypsy societies derive their cohesion from the force of collective awareness. Despite the diversity, the feeling of belonging to the same category of individuals is stronger than the sense of difference that divides them. Solidarity is buttressed by the flexibility of the society: constant travelling makes it possible to escape the ascendancy of the surrounding environment, and the ability to move on also helps to mitigate internal disputes. Tensions can be defused if one of two feuding families takes to the road. The absence of unity is in the very logic of Gypsy social organization. Flexibility is strength.

This does not mean that Gypsy rules are not strict. Solidarity and flexibility are backed up by an unbending notion of purity (and impurity) which governs most behaviour. Gypsies must behave in the Gypsy way and conform to Gypsy opinion. The deviant is declared impure and cast out. No one is prepared to cross the barrier of impurity, which is also the boundary of society, for to cross it is to become an outsider, a gadžo, with whom contacts must be limited and strictly controlled.

The gadžo, it must be remembered, is by definition polluted since he follows none of the rules for maintaining purity, and contact with the impure leaves indelible traces. Humanity is thus radically divided by the system of taboos related to purity.

The Gypsies assert their identity through opposition to non-Gypsies. The opposition is reciprocal, for Gypsies are people who are treated in a certain way by the gadže. The identity thus forged finds strength in resistance. Opposition to the gadže asserts Gypsy originality. If the hostile attitude of the gadže disappeared, it is not unlikely that the various groups that feel themselves 'Gypsy' would have neither the opportunity nor the need to come together in this way.

Apart from easily identified features like solidarity, flexibility, a rigid system of taboos, and opposition to the gadže, there are other, less tangible factors that help to hold society together. Among these is child-rearing, which from the earliest age orients the child towards the community. Gypsy children become used to generosity and sharing, and what might be called a continuum of kinship relations (no qualitative distinction is made, for example, between mother and aunt, or mother and grandmother) results in a community upbringing, protecting the child from the effects of any separation that may occur later. Space too is community-wide, without boundaries. At the level of the family, there is a continuum of dwelling, the essential room being a common living-room, with few or no individual rooms such as bedrooms.

What does it mean to be a Gypsy? Put the question to Gypsies, and you get a variety of replies. 'Being Gitan, a Traveller, a Gypsy, is most of all a way of *feeling* life, a way of living.' 'To me, when I say Gitan, it's a way of acting . . . I've never felt the need to be any more specific about it. I just feel . . .' 'Oh, when I run into somebody who is one, then yes, I feel I've got something, sort of automatically, in common with them. It's like I know them. With the gadže you feel nothing like that.' 'Being a Gypsy means feeling you're a Gypsy. At first there's no choice, you're born Gypsy. But then, faced with gadžo society, the choice becomes something real for a Gypsy. He's not an imaginary being, an image. He might adopt the fashion of the times, he's not afraid of appearances, because his life is somewhere else' [11]. Gypsy culture is based on indescribable and intangible ways of being, on ways of doing things which, however varied and ephemeral, must conform to custom. The way of doing things is part of the way of being, and the only really important thing about the objects of ritual is the ritual itself: there are no such things as Gypsy automobiles, but there is a Gypsy way of using them; there is no such thing as a Gypsy trade, but there are Gypsy ways of doing certain trades.

It is therefore not hard to understand why Gypsies have been able to absorb many features of the culture of their environment without weakening their own culture, for the borrowings have been used in an original, 'Gypsy' way.

The Gypsy identity is therefore powerful, and has been able to resist the vagaries of history. Gypsies who challenge it with deviant action tend to vanish into gadžo society and are obliterated from memory. Life-style is the key to the cohesion and survival of Gypsy society.

STRAFF DER HEYDE

3

GYPSIES AND NON-GYPSIES

Relations between Gypsies and non-Gypsies have never been untroubled. From the moment of their discovery of Western Europe in the fourteenth and fifteenth centuries, when they spilled into societies the state was seeking to organize and control, Gypsies were seen as intruders, nomads lacking hearth or home amidst local communities rooted in fixed and familiar soil. They aroused mistrust, fear, and rejection. Though they were few in number (often far less than 1 per cent of the population), they worried princes and peasants alike, and the way they were treated is indicative of the cultural values upheld by those among whom they lived. The measures taken against this handful of misfits down through the centuries speak volumes about the proclivities of the rulers of the societies in which they lived.

Central Government Action

From France to Czechoslovakia and from Spain to the Soviet Union, from the fourteenth century to the twentieth, it's the same story: whether aiming at rejection or assimilation, the policies adopted towards Gypsies were always negative. These policies were so similar that it is tiring to go through them all. But different types of attitudes towards Gypsies can be detected despite the apparently uniform hostility.

Expulsion
One of the most universally adopted policies has been for governments to expel Gypsies from the country. It is hard to

◁ Punishment for Gypsies, a
warning placard (18th century)

believe that such moves were unco-ordinated, for banishment was repeatedly prescribed in law after law and state after state over centuries: from the beginning of the sixteenth century to the middle of the twentieth in the case of France, for example. The most terrible punishments were laid down for failure to comply. Wooden panels in Germany and the Netherlands show a Gypsy hanging from a scaffold and a Gypsy woman being whipped—an artistic method of letting those still alive know what to expect. An edict of the Châtelet in Paris dealing with 'all those who call themselves Bohemians or Egyptians, their women, children, and following' stated that 'whenever they are met in any towns or villages' the alarm should be sounded and the authorities should 'hunt them down'. In many regions the sounding of the tocsin signalled open season on Bohemians— men, women and children—firearms being used in the event of resistance. Bounties were paid to those most skilled at capturing Bohemians dead or alive, and the profession of 'bounty-hunter' arose.

When the Gypsies appeared in the Netherlands in 1420, they were called Heiden (pagans) or Egyptenaren (Egyptians). Quickly rejected, they were 'so scorned as to be considered no more than parasites and foreign vagabonds of the worst sort, people with no rights at all . . . the killing of whom was seen as a boon to society' [126]. On 4 April 1525 Charles v issued an edict in Holland ordering all those calling themselves Egyptians to leave the country within two days. Fresh expulsion measures were taken in October 1533, and Gypsies were condemned for begging, chiromancy and magic [128]. But the Gypsies stayed on and repression got worse: confiscation of their property, forced labour, long prison sentences, whipping, branding. In the eighteenth century *Heidenjachten*, pagan hunts, were organized, terrible round-ups in which infantry, cavalry, and police took part [see 125]. In Denmark a picture of a Gypsy-hunting party organized on 11 November 1835 shows more than 260 people, including men, women and children.

Slovakia and the neighbouring regions had what might be called a tradition of welcoming Gypsies. Sigismund had issued a safe-conduct order in either 1417 or 1423 at Spiš castle in north-eastern Slovakia. King Matthias (in 1476 and 1487), King Vladislav (in 1492 and 1496), and several other kings wrote letters of commendation for Gypsies, who then tended to settle down and provide various services, acting as messengers, musicians, and smiths while continuing their fortune-telling and 'sorcery' in this hospitable country [see 57]. In 1523 Prague officially allowed nomads to stay, and several towns made them gifts in the sixteenth century. Given the harsh laws of neighbouring countries, significant numbers of Gypsy immigrants entered Slovakia, whose policy subsequently fell in line with that of other nations. In Prague on 7 January 1710 Joseph 1 issued an edict that all adult Gypsy men be hanged without trial and that boys and women be mutilated: the left ear cut off in Bohemia, the right in Moravia. Lodging or otherwise aiding Gypsies was punishable by up to six months' forced labour [127]. In 1721 the emperor Charles vi ordered that Gypsy men and women alike be killed, their children sent to orphanages. Five years later, the edict was renewed: now men were to be hanged, women and children under 18 to have their ears cut off and be banished; if they returned, they would be killed too. In 1740 punishments were decreed for any person aiding Gypsies [57; see also 34]. Whole groups were hanged or slaughtered. Signposts were set up along the roads showing a gallows with the caption: 'This is the punishment for Gypsies who trespass in Bohemia.'

Switzerland has a long tradition of persecuting Gypsies and nomads. From the beginning of the sixteenth century through the seventeenth, according to the orders of the Diet (the parliament), 'persons with no fatherland' were to be tortured or, as stipulated in 1580, set loose so that anyone who encountered them might kill them. Gypsy hunts were organized throughout the Swiss Confederation, as in Germany and the Netherlands. An ordinance passed in Berne in 1646 gave anyone the right 'personally to kill or liquidate by bastinado or firearms' Gypsy and Heiden malefactors. In 1727 Berne decree no. 13 reiterated that Gypsies were forbidden to stay and went on to stipulate: 'Gypsy men and women of more than 15 years of age shall have one ear cut off the first time they are caught . . . but if they are caught a second time they shall be sentenced to death' [100, p. 128]. 'Persons with no fatherland' were also sent to the slave galleys in Italy and France.

In the nineteenth century, French municipal authorities were ordered to register all nomads residing in their territory. Since the registration was set for a specific day, nomad hunts were organized in advance, their aim being to drive the undesirables into neighbouring districts. There were many tactical tricks. A local authority, for example, might summon the nomads the evening before the census and offer them a barrel of wine provided they drank it in the next district, all drunks thus being registered as part of the population of the neighbouring authority. Nomads were also bartered between districts [53].

In Germany, the tolerance with which Gypsies were met at their first appearance in Hildesheim in 1407 lasted less than half a century. The city of Frankfurt-am-Main drove them out in 1449 [79; see also 66]. By the end of the century the Reichstag— meeting in Landau and Freiburg in 1496, 1497, and 1498—had declared the Gypsies traitors to the Christian countries, spies in the pay of the Turks, and carriers of the plague. They were accused of witchcraft, kidnapping of children, and banditry. But the law had little effect, and it was renewed by the Augsburg Reichstag in 1500, at the request of the emperor Maximilian I. In 1531 the Augsburg Reichstag forbade the issuing of passports to Gypsies.

Since the Gypsies were not tolerated on German territory, they could be killed with impunity. Ferdinand I, seeking to show greater clemency, forbade the killing of women and children on sight, but the expulsion and extermination order was maintained for men. In Dresden in 1566 'two Gypsies seized after the expulsion order had come into effect were thrown from a bridge over the Elbe' [18, p. 54].

In 1579, on the pretext that German and foreign criminals were hiding among the Gypsies, Augustus, elector of Saxony, ordered the confiscation of their passports and banished them from his state. The Thirty Years' War gave people something else to think about besides nomads, but after the Peace of Westphalia, which divided Germany into some three hundred little sovereign states, each ruler took measures against the Gypsies. Laxity was not encouraged, and in 1652, when the local authorities in Bautzen allowed Gypsies into town to make purchases in preparation for a wedding, a magistrate fined the

Extract from *La cosmographie universelle*, Münster ▷

DE CES CHRESTIENS, QVI
sont vagabonds par le monde, lesquels on appelle
Egyptiens, diseurs de bonne auenture,
ou Sarrazins.

L'An apres la natiuité de Iesus Christ 1417. com-
mencerent à se monstrer en Alemagne, ie ne
sçay quelle maniere de gens, noirs, cuits au soleil,
vestus ordement, & salles en toutes leurs façons de
faire, sur toutes choses experts à larrecin, & princi-
palement les femmes, lesquelles nourrissent leurs
maris des larrecins, qu'elles font. Le commun peu-
ple en Alemagne les appelle Tartares ou Payens,
& en Italie on les nomme Cinganes. Ils honorent
le Duc, & les Comtes, qui sont entr'eux, lesquels
sont bien habillez : ils nourrissent des chiens à la
façon des gentilshommes, mais ils n'ont dequoy
chasser, s'ils ne l'empoignent par larrecin. Ils chan-
gent bien souuent leurs cheuaux, non obstant
la plus grand' partie d'entreux va à pied. Les femmes vont à cheual ou sur des iumens, portans leurs

les ẽmettent de d'au
regard des mains, &
dent à ceux qui les int
rs, ou combien d'enf
il y doiuent auoir, elle
leuse astuce dedans les
mandent, & les pinsen
ans, du temps que moy
ses, estant à Heydelber
paux de ces ruistres cv
racher cecy d'eux, qui
qu'ils se vantent auoir
ils me monstrerent vr
qu'ils auoyent impetr
Lindau, esquelles este
leurs ancestres auoyẽt
stienne pour quelque
estoyent retournez au
pres leur repentance
qu'autât d'annees que
esté en cest erreur des
aucun de toutes les fa
voyager par le monde
sement & exil, ils ob
che là. Mais il y a long
peregrinatió est passe,
cesse de trotter ça & là
uiner, & dire la bonn
proposoye cela, ils me
leur estoit fermé, ce e
ner en leur pays, com
nitence fust passé. Ie l
des, aux quelles ils re
i'ay honte de le mettr
beaucoup de bailleurs
simples par merueille
choses, qui ne sont poi
ne veirent iamais. l'
pendard de ceste belle
seil de leur comte, que
en leur pays, ils sont c

licts, & leurs enfans. Ils portent par tout des lettres
du Roy Sigismond, & de quelques autres princes,
à fin qu'ils puissent passer librement, & sans danger par les villes, & pays. Ils disent, que penitence

authorities heavily. In 1659 a group of Gypsies were exterminated in Neudorf, near Dresden. In 1661 the Elector Johann Georg II, again in Saxony, issued a decree imposing the death penalty on Gypsies captured in his territory. In the years that followed they were hunted down by cavalry. Everywhere they were stigmatized as undesirables and malefactors, an idle rabble.

After 1700 attempts were made to settle Gypsies and to split up families. In 1710 Frederick I, king of Prussia, condemned Gypsy men to forced labour, women to be flogged and branded, and children to be taken from their parents. Anyone harbouring Gypsies could be fined. Frederick Augustus, king of Poland and elector of Saxony, allowed the killing of anyone who resisted arrest. In 1721 the emperor Charles VI ordered the extermination of the Gypsies. In 1725 Frederick William I condemned any Gypsy over 18 caught in his territory, man or woman, to be hanged.

In the twentieth century (1905) the government carried out a census of Gypsies, both nomadic and settled, in Bavaria. The introductory remarks to the resulting report [see the study of it in 132] show that attitudes to nomads had not changed. Gypsies were described as a pest against which society had to defend itself by unrelenting vigilance. Any arrival or departure of Gypsies, indeed any incident involving them, had to be reported to the authorities. Citizens were advised to telegraph or telephone police headquarters in Munich, where a 'Gypsy information office' had been set up in March 1899. In 1926 the Bavarian parliament adopted a law designed 'to combat Gypsies, nomads and idlers', and the criminal commission of the *Länder* (provinces) endorsed the 16 July 1926 law aimed at suppressing the 'Gypsy plague'. A law passed on 12 April 1928 and an ordinance of 22 May 1928 placed the Gypsies under permanent police surveillance. All these acts were in violation of article 109, paragraph 3 of the constitution, which guaranteed equal rights for all. The German measures were similar to those taken by the French government around the same time: a census of nomads in 1895, followed by a law on their status in 1912, which compelled them to carry identity passbooks. This law remained in force in France until 1970.

Between 1933 and 1945, the years of Nazi rule in Germany,

the Gypsies faced an extermination campaign that went far beyond the murderous witch-hunts of earlier centuries. The Nazis considered them members of an inferior race, or of a mixture of inferior races (despite their Indo-European language), and therefore biologically and socially dangerous. All Gypsies in Germany were listed by Robert Ritter's institute (which had compiled more than thirty thousand genealogies by 1942), and restricted to their living areas. In 1938 a law was passed to counter the 'Gypsy threat', and deportations to Poland were organized in 1939 and 1940. The final chapter of Nazi policy towards the Gypsies opened with an order issued on 16 December 1942, supplemented by enforcement provisions in January 1943. On 1 March 1943 all the Gypsies in Germany, with a few exceptions, were arrested and deported, most of them to Auschwitz. More than twenty thousand Gypsies perished in this death camp. Similar measures were taken in the countries occupied wholly or in part by the German armies. It is estimated that between two hundred and fifty thousand and three hundred thousand Gypsies were exterminated. (The important role of French concentration camps, set up after the decree of 6 April 1940 and a circular of 29 April from the Ministry of the Interior to prefects, should also be noted. As C. Bernadac has said, 'The French state was ahead of the victorious Reich in the provisional, rather than the final, solution of the Gypsy problem' [13, p. 45]. He describes at length these French 'concentration camps', the term used by the authorities at the time. On the Nazi period and the Gypsies, see 13, 84, 56, 70, 137, and especially 63.)

Until 1947, in several regions of Germany, Gypsies coming out of concentration camps could be arrested and sent to labour camps under the terms of a 1926 law that placed Gypsies having no trade under police jurisdiction. As late as 1954 police authorities in Bavaria set up a special office, in contact with Interpol, to register Gypsies [reported by 138]. In the Cologne region, identity papers given to survivors of the concentration camps were withdrawn from Gypsies between 1950 and 1967 on the grounds that they could provide no written proof of their German nationality. They were instead given passports marked 'stateless' or 'of indeterminate nationality' [16, p. 15]. Under the Convention on the Status of Stateless Persons in force in Germany since January 1977, Gypsies cannot be deported, whereas nomads arriving from abroad can be refused entry—as had happened in September 1967, when forty-six Gypsies from Iran were stopped in Fürth while trying to cross into Germany from Czechoslovakia: for five days they were bounced from one police station to another, as neither European country was willing to accept them. The Iranian chargé d'affaires in Bonn finally had to repatriate them to Iran in a sealed bus.

Distressing situations continue to occur in Germany. One Auschwitz survivor whose tattooed number was clearly visible was refused entry to a campsite. 'This camp is not for you,' he was told. Another Auschwitz survivor, a Gypsy woman who asked permission to reside in her usual town, was summoned to a medical examination and found herself sitting opposite the doctor who had sterilized her in the camp [121]. A tabulation of French legislation on Gypsies from 1504 to 1803 (see below) shows that the French state was generally no more clement than the German.

The prime prohibition directed against Gypsies was usually residence (hence banishment as a punishment). But nomadism was itself often banned, and so was sedentarization, as Gypsies were often barred from settling or building houses and non-Gypsies were forbidden to sell to Gypsies. There were also bans on moving about in groups of more than three or four. Ultimately, then, it was the very existence of Gypsies that was prohibited. For several centuries the mere fact of being a 'Bohemian' in France was punishable by being sent to the galleys. The goal was to eliminate people targeted by these laws. Since they could not all be killed (except under the Nazi regime), other means were contemplated. At one point, for example, it was proposed to send them to an island in the Pacific or to their 'country of origin', which was unknown to the authors of the proposal. Failing this, some would be sent to people the colonies in the Americas, while others would populate the poor houses. Those who managed to escape would be perpetually on the run, committing an offence by the very fact of living as Bohemians. Anyone giving them alms, aiding them, or harbouring them risked heavy penalties, and in some periods the king could withdraw the judicial privilege of nobles guilty of these crimes.

Legislation Specifically Concerning the 'Bohemians' in France, 16th to 19th Centuries

(There are many other texts which deal with vagabondage, nomadism or begging, and therefore included the 'Bohemians' in their effects.)

Year	Prohibition	Punishment	Repeated offence or non-compliance
1504 (Louis XII)	Residence	Banishment	
1510 (Grand Council)	Residence	Banishment	Hanging
1539 (Francis I)	Residence	Banishment	Corporal punishment
1561 (Charles IX)	Residence	Banishment	Men: galleys and corporal punishment. Men, women and children: head shaved
1606 (Henry IV)	Gathering (max. 3 or 4)	Punishment as 'vagabonds and evil-doers'	
1647 (Louis XIV regency)	Being a 'Bohemian'	Galleys	

(continued)

Year	Prohibition	Punishment	Repeated offence or non-compliance
1660 (Louis XIV)	Residence	Banishment	Galleys or corporal punishment
1666 (Louis XIV)	Being a 'Bohemian'	Men: galleys. Women and girls: flogging, branding and banishment	
1673 (Louis XIV)	Residence	Banishment	Galleys
1682 (Louis XIV)	Being a 'Bohemian'	Men: galleys for life. Women: head shaved. Children: sent to poor house	Women: branded and banished
1700–16 1720/21/22 (Lorraine)	Begging, vagabondage in general	Banishment	Iron collars, branding and banishment
1719 and other years		Sentencing to the galleys is altered to deportation	
1723 (Lorraine)	Residence, gathering in the woods or main roads	Banishment: communities should gather, 'march in formation and open fire on them'	

(continued)

Year	Prohibition	Punishment	Repeated offence or non-compliance
1724 (Louis xv) Vagabonds and vagrants	Residence, nomadism, gathering of more than 4 adults	Adult men: galleys (5 years). Others: flogging and poor house	Galleys (9 years) and, for further repetition, in perpetuity; confinement (9 years) or in perpetuity
1764 Vagabonds and vagrants	Residence, nomadism	Adult men: galleys (3 years). Others: confinement in poor house (3 years), then choice of domicile and trade	
Year II	Giving or seeking alms	Fine to the value of two days' work, incarceration	
1802 (Basque country)	Residence, being a 'Bohemian'	Deportation failure	
1803 (Bonaparte)		Children, women, aged: to the poor house Young men: navy, army. Adult men: forced labour	
Various local and regional measures	Residence, being a 'Bohemian'	Removal, banishment, prison	

Ne uoila pas de braues messagers
Qui uont errants par pays estrangers.

Callot fec.

Jacques Callot, *Les Bohémiens* (17th century)

Who exactly were the individuals targeted by this expulsion policy? The laws designated them 'Bohemians'. But in five centuries that term was never defined. The laws, edicts, declarations, and ordinances sometimes lump together 'the poor, Bohemians, and vagrants', 'bands of Bohemians and brigands' 'Bohemians, vagabonds, vagrants and destitute foreigners',

'thieves and Bohemians'. The 'Bohemians' mentioned in all
these laws are in bad company. When they are cited alone, the
tone is pejorative: 'vagabond intruders calling themselves
Egyptians' (Louis XII, 1504); 'those commonly called Bohemians
or Egyptians' (Louis XIV, 1666); 'the sort of people adept only at
robbing others (Colbert, correspondence); 'people whose lives

are a kind of voluntary and perpetual banishment and who, driven from one province, cross blithely into another, where, maintaining their pattern, they continue to commit the same outrages' (declaration of 1764); 'foreign vagabonds known as Bohemians' (1864 circular). In a speech preceding the vote on the 1912 law in France, Senator Flandin spoke of 'ethnic vagabonds, Romanichals, Bohemians, Gypsies'. He continued: 'Their wretched caravan always carries a large tribe . . . They seem entitled to every privilege in our land . . . Terror in our countryside . . . suspicious caravaneers who, appearing to practise an alleged profession, trail their idleness and thieving instincts along the highways.'

This pejorative imagery, present in every country that legislated on the subject, gives few details about the people whose lives the law claimed to govern. But lawmakers were happy with it, and avoided the question of a definition whenever it was raised. In 1907, for example, when Deputy Fernand David rose to deplore the French government's weakness and impotence in dealing with 'Bohemians', no one in the National Assembly seems to have been able to define a Bohemian. The deputy, however, was unperturbed. 'The only problem', he said, 'is to find the solution.' And indeed stereotyped imagery had always served as the foundation for laws against Gypsies. The image was dark and indistinct, as it had been from the very beginning. When the first Gypsies appeared outside Mâcon in 1419 they were described as 'people of terrible aspect in their person, their hair, and otherwise and [who] lay in the fields like beasts'. In 1427 there is mention of 'witches who looked at people's hands' at the gates of Paris [62], while a source in Bologna in 1422 tells us: 'it must be noted that there is no worse brood than these savages. Thin and black, they eat like swine' [83].

Back in the fifteenth century these people—'horrible in their blackness', as Sebastian Münster described them in the *Cosmographia Universalis* [165]—were fixed in people's minds and then in laws, and so they have remained. No one knew where they came from or where they were going. Everywhere they were seen as useless troublemakers. The expulsion policy required a stigmatizing image, and it was provided right from the Gypsies' arrival. Lawmakers, who needed this image, cared neither to check its accuracy nor to modify it; on the contrary, they endorsed and even magnified it, using it as the basis and pretext for law.

But did all these laws offer any justification for the expulsion of Gypsies? The most common crime was the mere fact of being a 'Bohemian'. Many people were arrested and sentenced for 'calling themselves Bohemians', this being seen as a decision on their part which permitted them to lead a life of dissidence. In 1633, for instance, the 'self-styled Sebastien Lescuyer, of Egyptian or Boëme nationality', was condemned for having been 'found guilty of calling himself Egyptian, and on this pretext roaming the countryside'. Condemned as of 'Boëme nationality' he was perceived as inevitably dissident, and so was flogged, branded on both shoulders, and banished for life after serving 'the king in his galleys as a convict for the time and space of three years' [6, pp. 36–7]. A list of galley-slaves drawn up in 1739 shows that of ninety-four 'Bohemians' only three had been condemned for theft, acts of violence, or brigandage. The crimes of the others were listed as 'Bohemian according to the king's declaration', 'Bohemian and a vagabond', 'vagabond known as an Egyptian and Saracen', 'Bohemian and admitting to being so', 'vagrant Bohemian consorting with other Bohemians'. Some non-Bohemians were apparently sentenced for keeping bad company: 'dissolute vagabond consorting with Bohemians', 'following Bohemians and having dealings with them' [129, p. 179].

To be a Bohemian was to be likely to upset order, a crime meriting punishment. As a Lithuanian pastor said in 1787, 'Gypsies in a well-ordered state are like vermin on an animal's body' [63, p. 28]. Francis I complained in an edict of 1539 that they went 'as they pleased'. Order was what every 'well-policed' state sought; it was the pretext for all measures taken against anyone liable to disturb it. Gypsies were lumped together with witches and fortune-tellers, and later with the 'dangerous classes'.

Even before the arrival of Gypsies in Great Britain at the beginning of the sixteenth century, an English act of 1388 shows that wanderers were already regarded as 'suspicious persons

Varin, *Le ménage ambulant* (18th century)

living suspiciously'. This attitude helps to explain the various acts of parliament against 'Egyptians' (in 1530, 1554, and 1562), which enjoined them to abandon their 'evil, idle, and impious life and their company' and to take up a trade. Otherwise they would have to leave the country. In 1546 the English Navy was ordered to put some 'Egyptians' on a ship by force and send them to Boulogne or Calais [31]. Between 1720 and 1765 there were regular deportations to America and Australia [118].

For most of the five and a half centuries that Gypsies have been in Europe, they have been lumped together with vagabonds and vagrants, in laws and commentaries alike. In his *Mémoire sur les vagabonds*, for example, written in 1764, Le Trosne describes vagabonds as 'voracious insects who daily lay waste the wherewithal of cultivators. They are, quite literally, enemy troops who fan out as though in a conquered country, exacting levies under the name of alms' [66, quoted by 41, p. 79]. Some one hundred and fifty years later, Clemenceau described 'Bohemians' as 'exploiting and holding the populace to ransom and disturbing the tranquillity of the countryside by monstrous attacks'. Reville, a French parliamentary deputy, held that 'they live on our soil as in conquered territory', an assessment endorsed by Senator Flandin and Dubief, a former cabinet minis-

Raffet, *Famille Tsigane en voyage* (1839)

ter and chairman of the commission on vagabondage: 'with threats on their lips, they demand hospitality or hand-outs and are quick to avenge any refusal with a fire, sometimes even with murder'. Le Trosne urged the mounted constabulary and the populace to hunt the vagabonds down. Captures should be rewarded: 'A reward of ten pounds is given for a wolf's head. A vagabond is infinitely more dangerous to society' [66, quoted by 41, pp. 90–1]. In Spain, 150 years before Le Trosne, Sancho de Moncada penned a supplication to the king describing Gypsies as 'far more useless than the Moors. . . behaving only as wolves, thieving and fleeing'. 'There is no law', he wrote, 'obliging us to bring up little wolves who will inevitably attack cattle in the future' [80].

So the wolves had to be destroyed, with a clear conscience and for the greater good of society. The 'Bohemian profession' was incompatible with law and order.

The populace, who had a healthy fear of witches and sooth-sayers, did not at first bring pressure on the state to reject Gypsies. It was the central state, just beginning to take shape itself, that took the lead in repressing people who were con-sidered carriers of subversion and perversion regardless. 'Their existence helps to encourage those of criminal disposition, who hope that everything will be blamed on them', wrote the prefect of the Basses-Pyrénées in 1802. Gypsies therefore had to be expelled as a preventive measure. A Strasburg magistrate wrote at about the same time: 'I have no charges to prefer against these individuals, but their position is such that they must inevitably be tempted to commit crimes should the opportunity arise . . . They can only be dangerous.'

Although banishment was the clearest expression of the expulsion policy, it was neither the most practical nor the most economical. Since all countries were expelling Gypsies, there was nowhere for them to go, and hunting them down took time and money. Non-compliance and recidivism were common, and by banishing Gypsies the state lost labour-power. The exigencies of economics were soon felt. Capital punishment for repeat offenders was replaced by galley-slavery when manpower was short, and galley-slavery by transportation to colonies that needed settling. In the seventeenth century women were sent to the poor house instead of being banished, and later to factories with which the poor houses were often associated.

The Gypsies, moving about in their nomadic groups, were seen as physically threatening and ideologically disruptive. Their very existence constituted dissidence. The state therefore resolved to kill them or to drive them into neighbouring states (which then did exactly the same thing), or to colonies overseas. When, over the centuries, this tactic of expulsion proved limited or ineffective, the only alternative was to confine the dissidents: in prisons, in factories, or under daily police surveillance on the fringes of society. The unflattering portrait of Gypsies in legal documents and commentaries was simultaneously a justification for repressive laws and an excuse for their harshness, as the state cast itself as the protector of the people threatened by Bohemians. Its coercion thus reinforced its own hegemony and won acceptance of the social order it upheld.

Confinement and Forced Assimilation
Ultimately, it proved impossible to implement the policy of simple expulsion. Moreover, the gradual rise of humanistic ideas on the one hand and technocratic attitudes on the other

combined to provoke a shift in the authorities' policy towards Gypsies. In the main, local government continued to seek to move them on, but national states began to speak in somewhat different terms.

Through much of eighteenth-century Europe, Gypsies were considered a nuisance because they were nomads. The measures aimed at expelling Gypsies had been based on a repulsive image of the targeted group as inherently evil. The policy of confinement, however—paradoxically the first stage in a policy of assimilation—was instead based on the notion that people were not born Gypsies but became Gypsies by choice, by following a certain life-style.

Spain—a country that has always tried to bring Gypsies into the fold of its citizens—provides an example of how the policy of forced assimilation worked. In 1499 the decree of Medina del Campo encouraged the Gitanos to find a master and a trade and barred them from travelling in groups, upbraiding them primarily for roaming 'from place to place' without a trade. But by the beginning of the seventeeth century, the complaints had become more serious. In his *Discursos* of 1619, addressed to the king, Sancho de Moncada wrote: 'What is certain is that those who wander about in Spain are not Gitanos but swarms of idlers, lawless atheists with no religion, Spaniards who invented this mode of life or sect of Gitanismo, and who daily induct into it idlers and outcasts from all of Spain . . . Since no nation of Gitanos exists, let this name and its use disappear and be forgotten.' Philip III, in the same year, declared: 'Let those who desire to settle do so in towns or localities of a thousand persons or more, and let them cease to employ the dress, name, or language of Gypsies, and since they are not of a Gypsy nation, let this name and its use disappear and be forgotten.' Philip IV, in 1633: 'It was stated that those who call themselves Gitanos are Gypsies neither by origin nor by nature but have adopted this mode of life whose effects are so unsavoury . . . And to extirpate completely the name of Gitanos we decree that they no longer be called by that name, that no one dare use it henceforth, and that to do so be considered a serious offence and punished as such.' Charles II, in 1695: 'In order that there be no doubt about who it is that is to be considered Gypsies . . . we declare that any man or

woman apprehended in the costume or dress hitherto used by
this sort of people or proved to have used the language they call
jerigonza shall be considered a Gypsy. In like manner, so shall
those reputed to have been considered Gypsies in the places they
may have frequented or in which they may have resided, if at
least five witnesses so testify.' In 1746 it was decreed that 'no
difference is permitted from the manner of dress, behaviour,
language, and way of life of other vassals of the king, since,
having been born thus . . . it is not normal for them to appear
otherwise.' After the great round-up in Andalusia in 1749,
several Spaniards who had been arrested by mistake were not
released, since their way of life qualified them as Gypsies. In
1783 Charles III wrote: 'I declare that those called or calling
themselves Gypsies are not so by origin or nature and that they
come from no unwholesome root. This being so, I order them
one and all to cease to employ the language, clothing, and roving
mode of life in which they have hitherto indulged.'

The chart below lists the various orders issued to Gypsies in
Spain over three centuries and the penalties for failure to
comply. The measures taken were terrible indeed. Gypsies were
often given deadlines—of two or three months—to cease being
Gypsies. Failure to comply with the impossible was severely
punished, and repeat offenders could be branded or even put to
death.

The Gypsies fared no better under enlightened despotism.
Maria Theresa of Hungary and her son Joseph II attempted to
reform the Gypsies by means of lashes (twenty-five for Gypsies
caught speaking their own language), labour and forced settlement. Gypsy clothing was forbidden along with the language
and nomadism. Church attendance was compulsory and Gypsy
children were often taken away from their families. On one
December night in 1773, for example, all Gypsy children over 5
in the Palatinate of Pressburg and at Fahlendorf were trans-
ported to distant villages and assigned to peasants who brought
them up for a stipend of 12–18 florins a year. The children ran
away to rejoin their families, who took refuge in the mountains
or disappeared in the plains.

In 1782 Joseph II issued a 59-point edict reiterating his policy:
compulsory schooling for children and compulsory attendance

Spanish Legislation on Gypsies, 16th to 18th centuries

Year	Order	Punishment
1499	Find a trade and master, cease travelling together, within 60 days.	100 lashes and banishment. For repeat offenders: amputation of ears, 60 days in chains, and banishment. Third-time offenders to become slaves of those who captured them.
1525/28/34	Same order reiterated	Same penalties
1539	Same order, within three months. Travelling in groups of more than 3 forbidden.	6 years in the galleys.
1560 and others	Same. Travelling in groups of more than 2 forbidden. 'Dress and clothing' of Gitanos banned.	Up to 18 years in the galleys for those over 14. Later altered: for nomads, death; for settled people, the galleys.
Early 17th century	Identical measures by parliament or the king each year. Horse-dealing forbidden.	The populace may form armed groups to pursue Gypsies.
1611	Gypsy occupations must be connected with working the land.	
1619	Banishment of all Gitanos from the kingdom within 6 months or settlement in a locality with over 1,000 inhabitants. Dress, name, and language of the Gitanos banned.	Death.

(continued)

Year	Order	Punishment
1633	Same. Public and private meetings banned. Gitanos must merge with the rest of the population, undistinguished in any way. The name Gitano and Gypsy dress forbidden.	Men: 200 lashes and 6 years in the galleys. Women: banishment; 2 years exile, fine of 50,000 *maravedís*. A Gitano found outside the assigned locality becomes a slave to the apprehending person. If discovered with a firearm: 8 years in the galleys.
1695	Census of all Gypsies within 30 days; they must declare their trade, way of life, weapons, mounts, etc., then 30 more days to leave the kingdom or settle in a locality of over 200 inhabitants. Horses forbidden. Fairs and markets forbidden. Dress and language forbidden.	Men: 6 years in the galleys. Women: 100 lashes and banishment. Men: 8 years in the galleys. Women: 200 lashes and banishment. Banishment; 6 years in the galleys. Men aged 17 to 60: 6 years in the galleys. Men aged 14 to 17: imprisonment. Women: 100 lashes and banishment.
	Protection and lodging of Gitanos.	Nobles: fine of 6,000 ducats and half of legal expenses. Others: 10 years in the galleys.
1717	Same. Places of residence are set out: list of 41 localities.	
1726	Same. Gypsies forbidden to appeal against sentences of courts.	

(continued)

Year	Order	Punishment
1731	Frequent surprise visits to Gypsies' houses to check compliance with all articles Trade with Gypsies forbidden.	Fine of 200 ducats.
1745	Settlement in assigned places within two weeks.	Execution: 'It is legal to fire upon them and to take their life.' Churches no longer asylums. Armed troops to comb the countryside.
1746	Reference to 1717/27/31/38 Settlement in 41 localities, and 35 new ones added. Families must be dispersed: 1 for each 100 inhabitants, and only 1 per street.	
1749	Great round-up and various decrees. Separation of 'the bad and the good' through inquiries and witnesses' reports.	For the 'bad': public works; escapees to be hanged. Motherless girls sent to poor houses or into service for honest people. Older girls and wives of sentenced men with children under 7 to be 'educated in Christian doctrine and the holy fear of God' and sent to factories.
1783	Reiteration of previous orders: dress, way of life, and language forbidden, settlement compulsory, within 90 days. The name Gitano forbidden, to be removed from all documents. Restrictions on trade and place of residence lifted.	Branding. For repeat offenders: 'death, with no appeal'.

at religious services. Gypsy language, clothing, and music were forbidden.

The enslavement of Gypsies in the Romanian principalities, which ended only in 1856, is the worst case of enforced restriction. Here, from the fourteenth century onwards, Gypsies were not expelled but instead became slaves of the state, the clergy, or the lords. The master had the right to beat and chain them. They were worse off than the 'Bohemians' in Western Europe: sometimes chained hand and foot, or even by the neck; hung over smoke as a punishment; thrown naked into snow or icy rivers. Women were separated from their husbands, children sold off and scattered throughout the country, sometimes exchanged between princes as presents. Newspapers in the middle of the nineteenth century were full of announcements of public sales of Gypsies. *Luna*, published at Agram, announced in 1845, for example: 'By the sons and heirs of Serdar Nicolai Nica of Bucharest, for sale: 200 Gypsy families. The men are mainly locksmiths, goldsmiths, boot-makers, musicians, and peasants. Not less than five families per lot. Payment facilities.' The Civil Code originally stipulated that Gypsies arriving from abroad were the property of the state. It was also specified that every Gypsy was automatically born a slave and that the child of a Gypsy slave was a slave.

In more recent times, Gypsies have also faced oppression and forced assimilation elsewhere in Eastern Europe. In Czechoslovakia, law no. 117 of 1927 prohibited Gypsy nomadism and barred nomads from 'leading the life of Gypsies'. 'Gypsy identity cards' were introduced as a means of control over this group living on the fringes of society. And 'by court order children under 14 may be taken from their families and placed in children's homes or with respectable families' [see 113]. Hatred of Gypsies eventually led to pogroms.

Czechoslovakia's policy after the second world war can be divided into several periods. From 1948 to 1957 there was no real policy at all. Other problems were more pressing, and Gypsies were seen as victims of capitalism: the advent of communism would settle the 'Gypsy problem'. Ten years later, however, the 'problem' had not disappeared, and the government resolved to deal with it under four watchwords: sedentary settlement, assimilation, labour, and schooling. Law 74 of 1958 on the permanent settlement of nomads banned nomadism. The law was applied with considerable brutality. The police killed the Gypsies' horses and took the wheels off their wagons and caravans to stop them travelling. Anyone living a nomadic life was considered a vagrant, unemployed and therefore having an illicit income; to remain a nomad was punishable by prison terms of six months to three years [see 133]. Special schools were set up as a stop-gap measure until Gypsy pupils could go to ordinary classes. The government also set great store by the educational role of military service, which lasts two years, and in the jobs specially reserved for Gypsies in state enterprises [76]. Many long-term assimilation programmes were drawn up, their implementation followed by floods of statistics. There were commissions and expert officials aplenty, and a host of figures seemed to prove that the programme was being successfully implemented.

Although they were quite numerous (some three hundred to three hundred and fifty thousand in all), representing nearly 10 per cent of the population, in some districts in eastern Slovakia, Gypsies were not recognized as a national minority. They were therefore not considered an ethnic group, and the authorities saw their language as no more than an impoverished jargon. They were defined by their way of life, not by their cultural identity. Those who seemed to lead lives like other citizens were no longer considered or counted as Gypsies [35]. The state radio commented that Czechoslovakia 'could not boast of achieving a salutary cultural revolution if thousands of comrades were allowed to live in primitive conditions and with no culture' [quoted in 133]. Yet the 'Gypsy problem' remained. Moreover: 'Socialist society not only facilitates but directly requires the integration of the Roma. Any population group that behaves in an unexpected manner, that does not conform to the model, disturbs the system of central planning, one of the fundamental principles of socialism. The integration of the Roma takes place in two basic areas: comprehensive schooling of children and putting men to work in non-Gypsy collectives' [59, p. 45].

A new period opened in 1965, with the creation of a government committee for Gypsy questions and a number of special commissions. Assimilation was still the main theme, but it was now thought that the process would be more rapid and effective if the Gypsies were dispersed. Slovakia, one region that still had many nomads at the end of the second world war, was to be cleared of its large Gypsy concentrations, whose inhabitants would be sent to Czech areas with fewer Gypsies. A study was commissioned from the Academy of Sciences and the Gypsies were duly classified into three categories according to their degree of 'culture', type of habitation, and presumed receptivity to assimilation:

1. The most advanced Gypsies (whose culture approximated that of the people among whom they lived): they were settled and had regular employment.
2. Gypsies who aspired to upward mobility.
3. Gypsies who were not ready for social and cultural assimilation in the near future.

Gypsies of the first category were chosen to be transferred to Czech lands [113]. According to circular no. 502, the dispersion represented 'a planned and organized migration of Gypsies from certain districts of Slovakia to certain districts of Bohemia designated in advance according to plan. Any unplanned, unorganized, and unapproved movement by a Gypsy (or a family) between the two districts shall be considered an undesirable transfer of Gypsies and inevitably rejected. It will then be necessary to send the Gypsy (or family) back to the place of origin at the expense of the district authority or person who permitted the transfer.' [Bulletin on 'Principles of Organization of the Dispersion and Transfer of Gypsies to Eliminate Gypsy Concentrations, in Accordance with the Decision of the Party and Government', Ministry of Finance, no. 122/14336/67, quoted in 58.]

This plan failed too. It ran counter both to the 'natural' migration patterns of Gypsies, who adapt better to the conditions of particular regions, and to the wishes of the hostile local populations who had been asked by the authorities to 'welcome' the Gypsies. The Gypsies deported under the plan either went back where they came from or were followed by their entire extended families, thus creating another of the concentrations against which the government claimed to be fighting. Bureaucratic delays and bottle-necks did not make things easier. Compulsory schooling and job integration didn't work either, partly because of the authoritarian way they were carried out and partly because of opposition from non-Gypsies in the schools and factories. In 1968 the magazine *Russkaia Misl* published an article by S. Sarfenov which condemned Czechoslovakia's failure in this field—of all the communist countries, it had had the least success in dealing with the Gypsy problem.

After the transfer programme's failure to break up the large Gypsy camps, it was proposed instead to improve the living conditions of Gypsies wherever they were. A new policy was sought.

In 1968 and 1969 Gypsies began organizing and founded two associations, one for the Slovak and the other for the Czech lands [see 69, pp. 164ff.]. In 1973, however, the Party banned Gypsy associations on the grounds that the population was not a recognized national minority. The idea of using Romany in schools was also abandoned, even though the Ministry of Education had commissioned several books. In the late seventies the Charter 77 group denounced violations of the rights of Gypsies in Czechoslovakia, charging that children had been taken from their families and placed in institutions so as 'to remove them from the influence of the ethnic group to which they belong'. And: 'Equally appalling is the sterilization of Gypsy women. In some districts this has become a common practice, and the success of officials is measured by the number of women they have convinced to get sterilized [quoted by *Monde gitan*, no. 47, 1979].

Local Government Action

Whatever the policies towards Gypsies adopted by central governments, it is at the local level that these policies have always been implemented—or not implemented. Regardless of what the state may say, it has always been the local authorities that have intervened most directly in the lives of the Gypsies. Here

Checking identity papers, France ▷

the record is, if anything, even more uniformly shoddy. Forcing Gypsies out has been the watchword.

When a hundred Gypsies arrived at the gates of Paris in 1427, the city sent them on to Pontoise in less than a month. The year before, the city authorities of Grap had paid three citizens to act as watchmen while 'the Saracens' were in town [129, p. 19]. Later on, citizens were sometimes summoned by alarm bells to defend their towns or hunt down 'Bohemians', with rewards for any captures. From the fifteenth century onwards, wounding or killing a Bohemian was a pardonable offence, even when Gypsy groups held passports from the king.

Sometimes, however, groups of Gypsies bearing letters of recommendation from this or that king, or a papal bull certifying them as pilgrims, were well received. Once alms-giving days were over and stories about pilgrimages were no longer believed, there was still one non-violent method of getting rid of Gypsies: a gift of food or money in exchange for their 'moving on' or 'passing through'. Negotiations were sometimes held in the presence of a lawyer. In exchange for a gift, the captain of the 'Egyptians' would agree to take his group through, make sure that no wrongdoing occurred, and promise not to come back within a certain period, usually a year. A *modus vivendi* emerged. For a few pounds or a fistful of *deniers*, the local authorities would buy a slice of tranquillity. The rejection underlying this sort of perverted alms-giving was obvious enough, and the Gypsies responded by making the most of the fear they rightly or wrongly aroused. Once people got over their initial surprise, and ceased to marvel at the extraordinary colourful groups of long-haired campers who appeared at the beginning of the fifteenth century, they were inclined to try to maintain order and make deals. In 1603 Jehan de la Grave, 'captain of a company of Egyptians', stated before a notary that he had 'received one *ecu* from the community of Lachau, given to him by Jehan Michel, one of the consuls in that place, which they have given him not to return to that place and to go elsewhere'. In September 1636 the village of Bras, near Saint-Maximin gave '20 *sous* to the Bouemiens. The said 20 granted to make the Indians depart this place' [129, pp. 67–8].

The populace was no longer curious about the bizarre, but worried about the unusual.

Outright Rejection

Local authorities in the twentieth century have various ways of making the Indians leave. Outright rejection of Gypsies and nomads is among the most common. In Saint-Brieuc in France the street-sign marking Place de la Liberté stands opposite one that says 'No parking for nomads and those with no fixed address'. In 1968 a meeting of the town council in Le Pouliguen decided to develop a site to accommodate 750 campers, for the exclusive use of tourists. The same meeting emphasized that there would be no room for nomads: 'The council requested that it be exempt from the legal obligation for municipalities to make provision to put up itinerants and passing nomads for twenty-four hours' (*L'Eclair de Nantes*, 11 March 1968). Back in the sixteenth century people were afraid that Gypsies carried the plague; in the twentieth they are seen as trouble-makers who should be kept out.

Apart from simply ordering Gypsies and nomads to move on, local authorities have sometimes expelled them by force, arms in hand. Legislation allowing this is occasionally already on the books. Back in 1646, for example, an ordinance against Gypsies and other Heiden was adopted at Berne: citizens were granted the right 'personally to kill or liquidate' suspicious persons 'by bastinado or firearms' [100, p. 128].

An ordinance passed by the town council of Aachen on 25 June 1728 condemned the Gypsies to death:

> We, citizens, patricians, and council of the free imperial city and royal seat of Aachen, enjoin one and all to take notice of the present edict. It has long been shown that, in our territory as in neighbouring countries, armed bands of Gypsies, along with all varieties of vagabonds without masters, have been committing thefts . . . Unable further to tolerate the presence of such rabble in our district of Aachen, we have solemnly decided to proceed against them as disturbing peace and public tranquillity, following the example of measures adopted in neighbouring lands.

Consequently, in our council held today we have decided to eradicate these scoundrels. If any such Gypsies, armed bands of rogues, or other groups of vagrants are discovered in the territory of Aachen, we must be informed at once that the militia required to repress them be despatched against them, which militia shall immediately be mustered by its captain or lieutenant. Protection shall be sought from the said militia and the hunt shall be pressed zealously to the ringing of bells. Captured Gypsies, whether they resist or not, shall be put to death immediately. However, those seized who do not resort to counter-attack shall be granted no more than half an hour to kneel, if they so wish, beg God Almighty to forgive them their sins and to prepare themselves for death' [reported in 18, p. 55].

More than two and a half centuries later, local authorities are still adept at showing Gypsies how unwelcome they are, as the following two testimonies show. The speakers are Gypsies talking about France.

I would like to tell you how we are treated on the road. Listen to this. Eight years ago my mother was very sick; she was in B. in the Dordogne when a doctor recommended that she should have several teeth out. Since she was pretty sick, we stopped at the fairground, but not for long, as it turned out. A police van arrived in ten minutes. They told us to leave. They said we had to be at least 7 km from town. Then we drove back in just one car and pulled in at the dentist's. Since she had coronary thrombosis, I went with her, taking my brothers and two of my cousins, in case anything happened. She's our mother, after all, so that's the least we could do. Well, the police happened to come down the street again. They ran at us to ask for our papers, screaming so loud that people stopped, maybe thinking we were robbers. I was really ashamed. I said we would show them our papers but they should at least be polite. So then they started hitting us and took us to the police station, and as we were coming in, the captain asked what was going on. They said to us: 'This is our country here.' Then three or

Gypsy encampment, France ▷

four of them started swinging and they stuck us in a cell for an hour when we should have been taking care of our sick mother. That's how the world treats us. (*Etudes tsiganes*, no. 1, 1966, p. 9.)

These days we're checked three times every hundred kilometres or so: papers, files, three hours at a time. Even our trailers and the lorries are searched. They open the doors to see if we're carrying alcohol . . . One day a doctor told us not to leave with sick kids. Even though the landowner agreed to let us stay, the guards drove us out. It's like we were Indians in America in the 1880s or something . . . The local authorities throw us out, and five or six gendarmes come along with vans. We were in Belfort for half a day when they showed up with machine-guns. (*Monde gitan*, no. 26, 1973 p. 5.)

Large groups of Gypsies who stop for any length of time are frequently expelled. In Noisy-le-Grand in November 1965, for instance, about two hundred families were driven out by policemen with dogs, and the following autumn several thousand men in Rosny-sous-Bois returned home from work to find that their makeshift but well-kept homes had been razed by building workers. Everything inside had been destroyed and their wives and children sat amid the ruins. A construction company had plans to build on the vacated site, but the occupants had been given no notice. The local chief of police sent a laconic explanatory letter to the Movement Against Racism and Anti-Semitism and for Peace: 'I have the honour to inform you that the measures taken with regard to this encampment were not meant to expel the occupants but to prevent their numbers growing.'

Actions like these destroy family structures and produce inevitable consequences: alcoholism, psychiatric hospitalization, and children being taken into care because of poor housing conditions [see 23, 67].

Indirect rejection
Outright rejection and violent expulsion are not the only tech-

niques employed by local authorities to get rid of Gypsies and nomads. There is also indirect rejection, which shuns violence in favour of setting impossible conditions for residence. This tactic affords several advantages for those who adopt it. Its classic symbol is the picture of two signs, standing side-by-side and bearing arrows pointing in the same direction. One says 'Site reserved for nomads', the other 'City dump'.

Then there is the health and vaccination technique, whereby the local council adopts a by-law with wording something like this: 'Whenever the persons named in article 1 (people with no fixed address or residence) arrive in the city limits to camp or park, they shall demonstrate with a duly authorized certificate that they have undergone the required vaccinations and re-vaccinations, failing which they shall submit to immediate vaccination or revaccination or else leave the city limits.' Tourists and other passers-by are not, of course, subject to this check.

Throughout France—to take the example of just one European country—instances of harassment are legion. There is a campsite in Argentan ringed by a 7-ft.-high wall with a single narrow opening, making it a virtual ghetto. Villedomer (Indre-et-Loire) has a 2,600-sq.-ft. site that can be used by no more than two cars for forty-eight hours. In Monthiers and Bézu-le-Guéry (Aisne), 'Nomads are permitted to stop, but the city council has no site.' In Brécy, in the same *département*, 'Nomads are forbidden to stop anywhere within the city limits. During the pea and bean harvest, nomads shall be permitted to stop on the roads known as Vingt Argents or de la Justice.' In Coincy, 'Stopping and camping by nomads are permitted only at the place known as Le Fond de Sorel. The period of stopping or camping at the said site shall not exceed two months (August–September), for the duration of seasonal work.' The local economy has its needs, as in Saintes-Maries-de-la-Mer, where Gypsies are expelled immediately after the pilgrimage. In Chierry, also in the Aisne, 'vagabonds, nomads, caravaneers, and Romanichals' are prohibited from stopping, whereas 'itinerants with proof of occupation' are allowed, although 'it is expressly forbidden for the said persons to be accompanied by children under 16 years of age'. In Nogent-l'Arthaud the law permits 'a stop of twelve hours by day or a single night', pro-

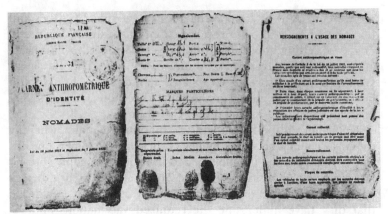

Identity papers, France

vided a request has been duly made at the town hall, which is closed on Saturday afternoons and all day Sundays. (The examples of the Aisne appeared in *Monde gitan*, no. 35, 1975.)

In Pouzac (Hautes-Pyrénées), stopping is permitted only at night along a road. In Bayonne, a by-law passed on 13 September 1972 allows nomads to stop only at a place called Chemin de l'Estanquet, which can hold two caravans at most. A mayoral decree of 23 May 1971 in Fauverney (Côte-d'Or) restricted stopping to twenty-four hours, on payment of a fee of 30 francs on arrival. The stay may be extended if a second fee is paid. The fee tactic is a favourite in Switzerland, where stopping places for Gypsies and Travellers are practically non-existent and the law allows the cantons to set the fees for licences to carry on trades. Cantons that want to keep Gypsies out set high fees: for example, 90 Swiss francs a week, during which hawking is allowed for only four days, plus a daily charge for getting the licence stamped at the police station. A licence issued by one canton is not valid in the others [16, p. 13]. The director of a psychiatric clinic in Chur had this to say about Gypsies: 'To protect peace in Switzerland it would be better to lock them up in psychiatric asylums and perhaps simply put them in prison' [reported in 109].

All these tactics make it possible to keep up a humanistic front. It is no longer the eighteenth century, when in Germany, the Netherlands, Czechoslovakia, or Switzerland wood carvings showing a Gypsy being flogged or hanged were posted on the outskirts of towns. The enamelled sign-board has replaced the wooden billboard, the written word stands in for crude painting, and the deterrent fine has ousted corporal punishment.

Indirect rejection keeps consciences clear and fits in with the assimilation policy of central governments. The velvet subtlety of the administrative language of central government gives way to grotesque word games at the local level, to regulations framed deliberately to permit abuse.

Famous Cases of Rejection: France
Rejection of Gypsies is sometimes considered excessive not because of its violence or severity, but because of its visibility. Occasionally the mass media, and consequently national public opinion, become alerted to the doings of local authorities or individuals. More-or-less routine acts of rejection then become celebrated cases. This may occur after the formation, say, of a so-called defence committee by the inhabitants of a district or town who oppose the establishment of facilities for nomads; the inhabitants may either support the rejectionist stand of their elected representatives, or criticize it if it goes against their own determination to reject the nomads. Citizens of the district of Longpré (Amiens), for instance, issued a communiqué, published in *Le Courrier picard*, demanding that nomads be sent away: 'When will the responsible authorities understand that decent people, sick of the irresponsibility and permissiveness that seem to typify our times, may finally resort to direct or collective action? Having already long contemplated defending themselves, they may also prove capable of taking risks and launching reprisals, under the old adage that the best defence is a good offence.' In Toulouse in 1973 it was proposed to rehouse some families from the Ginestous shanty-town in new buildings. The prospective neighbours formed an 'association for the protection of the interests of Saint-Martin-de-Touch' and the case dragged on for almost two years, finishing up before the Council of State. The same things happen in other regions.

In 1971 in Dung, in the Doubs region of France, a Gypsy family which had requested public housing was rejected on the grounds that 'it is impossible to accommodate Gypsies in the midst of the population'. 'Perhaps they are not bad people,' the mayor explained, 'but no one wants them here.' In Helfranz-kirch in 1968 the city council refused to house a family with ten children. The mayor wrote to the Mulhouse sub-prefect: 'The Helfranzkirch council wonders what degree of responsibility the sub-prefect intends to impose on the council. To settle this family of Gypsies in the city, whether by granting them a plot of land or by offering them housing would be to attract still more nomads.' The mayor told the local newspaper that if the sub-prefecture forced him to keep this family, the entire council would resign (*L'Alsace*, 27 January 1968). In March, after an appeal from the prefect, he replied that 'the council will stand by its position, believing that a family belonging to an itinerant social group cannot be forced on the city.' A few years earlier, the mayor had sent a tractor to tow the family's trailer out of the city to a cold and unhealthy site more than 1,500 yards from a water supply and 3 miles from the school [27, p. 93].

In Schalkendorf a Gypsy family had purchased an old farm. When the family moved in, the local population was up in arms. Traders refused to sell to the Gypsies and parents took their children out of school when the five Gypsy children began attending classes. The town council finally decided to buy the house at a high price, but feared that the prefecture would not approve the purchase. In the end the council acted through an agency, offering more than three times the price the Gypsies had paid. Faced with the hostility of their neighbours, the family accepted the sum.

In November 1980 there was a similar case in Mertzwiller, again in the Bas-Rhin. Gypsy families took their children out of school to protest at the council's refusal to grant permission to install bathroom and toilet facilities on their site. Here rubbish was not even collected and there were so many rats that the Gypsies had to mount a night guard to keep them away. Finally the sole water tap froze. 'We can't even wash our children any more, and then people say they stink,' the Gypsies complained. The deputy mayor still refused the permit for toilet facilities for these Gypsies, whose 'rapid growth threatens to distort the face of Mertzwiller in the near future'. (AFP, 22 November 1980.)

In 1974 in Hoerdt, a town of 3,200 near Strasburg, a family that had been settled on the edge of the town for some fifteen years suddenly left its spot. One of the sons had stolen a car and some local men had invaded a campsite, threatening the Gypsies. Their shacks were fired on during the night. The mayor seized this golden opportunity and, accompanied by the village constable and with the support of the population, had the hut and a caravan burned down, with clothes, mattresses, and other belongings still inside. The dogs and cats were killed and the site bulldozed. The mayor then declared that he had done 'his duty as mayor responsible for order and public cleanliness'. He enjoyed popular support, and the backing of many other mayors in the region as well. The family fled to a neighbouring town, Drusenheim, where they set up a tent. The prefecture, claiming to be helping them, offered them better tenting! But the mayor of Drusenheim expelled the family, with its small children, in sub-zero conditions. The state prosecutor is reported to have written to the Guardian of the Seals on 4 March 1974 asking him not to pursue the matter 'so as to avoid inciting violence in the area because of nomads' (*Monde gitan*, no. 29, 1974, p. 2). The family had no option but to move on. They returned to Hoerdt on 6 March but were again expelled by the mayor. The mayors of neighbouring towns followed suit.

Incidents like these, all of which occurred in France, are common in other countries too: Britain, Ireland, Germany, Spain—scarcely any state is free of them [for an overall analysis in Europe see 71].

The Machinery of Rejection: Examples from Britain

Government policy on Gypsies is often flagrantly ambivalent. While central government preaches assimilation in humanistic terms, Gypsies are nevertheless invited to move on, under the pretext of maintaining order and safeguarding public health. The whole body of provisions and regulations on camping and stopping can make life a Kafkaesque nightmare for nomads, and the weapons central government offers local authorities contradict the talk of tolerance and assimilation. Britain is a case in point.

In 1959, section 127 of the Highways Act prohibited Gypsies from encamping on a highway. The prohibition was directed explicitly and solely against Gypsies: if two caravans, one be-

Horse-fair, England

Caravans near Huntingdon, England

Roadside stop near Appleby, England

At the horse-fair, England ▷

longing to a Gypsy and the other to a non-Gypsy, encamped side by side, only the Gypsy was in breach of the law. In March 1967 the High Court, ruling on an appeal against the racist and discriminatory character of section 127, found that parliament had in fact made no reference to race in drafting the law. A Gypsy was therefore to be defined as 'a person leading a no-madic life with no fixed employment and no fixed abode' [52; 1, p. 178]. In the Caravan Sites Act of 1968 Gypsies are defined by their 'nomadic way of life'. The 'nomadic life' has itself never been defined by any national court, but two local courts ruled that a Gypsy who purchases a site is no longer a nomad and therefore no longer a Gypsy. By contrast, an individual who purchases a caravan and installs it without permission thereby becomes a Gypsy, since he or she knows that this illegal act will lead to expulsion and therefore to a nomadic life [64, p. 2].

In 1960 the Caravan Sites and Control of Development Act established the principle of permission to camp and gave local authorities the power to provide sites for Gypsies. Ultimately, however, the provisions of the act became weapons in the fight against nomads: the new power to regulate and thus to prohibit encampment gave a legal stamp to acts of expulsion, and most local authorities were in no hurry to provide sites for nomads. One member of parliament understood this and took an interest in the fate of nomads. In December 1961 Norman Dodds gave a five-hour speech in the House of Commons during which he described the facilities provided for Gypsies in England and Wales as 'the worst in the world' and argued that the 1960 law was making them even worse. He pointed out that the House of Commons library contained information on the most obscure of African tribes but nothing at all about the situation of Gypsies in England. Local authorities were concerned only with the num-ber of complaints against Gypsies from the public. He castigated the ineptitude of the 1960 law, which would penalize a farmer who tried to accommodate a caravan on his own land if he needed Gypsy labourers. The government seemed to respond to this speech, and a 1962 Home Office circular to local authorities stated that Gypsies have the 'right to follow their traditional mode of life'. Councils were encouraged to provide sites. Two years later, however, only four of the sixty-two counties of

England and Wales had provided a site [see 42].

The 1968 Caravan Sites Act requires local authorities to provide sites for encampment. Article 6, dealing with 'duties of local authorities to provide sites for Gypsies', says that they must 'provide adequate accommodation for Gypsies residing in or resorting to their area'. But the act does not define 'adequate accommodation' and in practice Gypsies' requirements are woefully underestimated. Moreover, in exchange for their obligation to provide sites, local authorities were given the right to prohibit camping in other places and to remove offenders, by force if necessary. Anyone obstructing such removal can be questioned, cautioned, and even arrested: 'A constable may arrest without warrant any person found committing an offence under this subsection' (article 11 of the amended act).

The 1968 act was meant to be assimilationist. One of the implementing circulars (23 August 1968) stated: 'It is hoped that in the long term the Gypsies will become completely integrated among the settled population.' A definition follows: 'The word "Gypsies" describes persons of nomadic habit of life, whatever their race or origin, but does not include members of an organized group of travelling showmen, or of persons engaged in travelling circuses, travelling together as such' (article 16 of the act). The *cultural* aspect is ignored, the emphasis is on the social 'problem', to be solved by sedentarization [see 2, pp. 5–23, 155–71; see also 119].

Despite the government's request to local authorities, the latter did not set up sites. In general, they have acted only on those parts of the law that suit them, using only those articles in the 1968 act that empower them to evict Gypsies. In the West Midlands, for example, it is estimated that between 1969 and 1975 the districts spent £1 million on removing and driving out nomads, and digging trenches or building fences round open spaces to prevent nomads gaining access to them. During the same period, sites were found for a total of only forty-five families, who thus gained the legal right to camp [96, p. 8]. Several years later, the Cripps Report compared the number of Gypsy families with the number of places on designated campsites and found that as of 1977 three-quarters of all families had no lawful place [29]. According to the Criminal Law Act of 1977, if Gypsies stop on a private road serving a dwelling, they can be arrested without a warrant. Under the Caravan Sites Act of 1960, if they stop on a site that belongs to them for more than two consecutive nights, they need planning permission and a site licence. Both of these are difficult to obtain and, in Britain as elsewhere, may be refused in the name of environmental protection or town-planning regulations that are no less vague. The police act quickly during evictions: caravans are attached to a tractor or Land Rover, and serious accidents sometimes occur, with children still inside being severely injured or burned [95; 63, p. 197; 2, p. 13].

Even when space is available on one of the legally designated sites, there are many petty harassments:

> A travelling caravan cannot enter a site and occupy an empty spot. The owner must, for example, go to the office in the town hall on Mondays between 2 and 4 p.m., fill in a form, pay four weeks' rent in advance and a deposit of £50, undertake to obey the rules of the site, show a certificate that his dog has had the required vaccinations and that his caravan has an electrical safety certificate . . . Once he is on the site, he must park his van with its load in special parking places that he cannot see from his caravan. He cannot work on the site or even unload his van. In the evening he cannot light a fire outside. The police visit the site regularly to take down the numbers of the cars, and from time to time families are awakened at 6 o'clock in the morning to see who is sleeping in each caravan. The laws governing scrap metal (the Scrap Metal Dealers Act of 1964, the Litter Acts of 1957 and 1971, the Civic Amenities Act of 1967, and the Public Health Act of 1936), which are used by the police against nomadic Gypsies, are applied even more strictly to these newly sedentarized people. With no possibility of earning his living, the newly sedentarized person cannot afford this new life. Electric heating is expensive, the older children have to go to school, their uniforms have to be paid for, and at the same time they have to forgo the money they could earn by working. Several families have left the municipal sites: others stay

Gypsy van in West Sussex, 1949

there, sad, remembering the past, living on social security
and comparing their lot to that of the American Indians in
the reservations [64, pp. 4–5. For a detailed analysis of
policies pursued in England and Wales, see 1].

Scotland's policy is similar to that of the rest of Britain. Until
the mid nineteenth century, the authorities simply rejected
Gypsies. Then a movement for assimilation through sedentarization arose. The Trespass (Scotland) Act of 1865 and the
Roads and Bridges (Scotland) Act of 1878 prohibited free camping, well in advance of the English laws of 1960 and 1968. A
committee set up in 1918 recommended sedentarization (a
house and a piece of land to work) as a means of integrating the
Gypsies into the settled population. It was hoped that education
would make children 'normal' rather than nomads. One current
official publication points out that if the laws were enforced,
nearly all nomads would be in an illegal situation [45; see also 46
and 99].

At bottom, the way Gypsies are treated has less to do with laws
than with the state of mind shaped by myths and stereotypes.
Government instructions mean little. Rejection is still an every-

day experience. Gypsies are regarded as potential thieves and trouble-makers, suspicious characters, perennial felons by the very fact of failing to comply with laws that for centuries have banished them, condemned them to the galleys or the scaffold. Centuries ago, local authorities rarely took account of the royal letters of protection carried by certain groups of Gypsies. In the twentieth century fear still holds sway, along with the attitudes that flow from it.

The image of Gypsies as forged by non-Gypsies has done much to incite a fear that in turn serves to justify and inspire rejection. Up to the twentieth century Gypsies were held responsible for 'ravages and disorders', 'pillaging and sacking'. Since Gypsies were usually lumped together with vagabonds and vagrants, with armed deserters from royal armies and highwaymen, the term 'nomad' or 'Gypsy', even in our own century, is itself tainted by misdeeds attributed to those they were confused with. The standard stereotype is based on a mixture of vague fear and superstition that can be traced back to tales of well-poisoning, the spread of plague, crop-burning, secret treasure troves, witchcraft, and healing hands—all projections of the fantasies of bygone ages, stacked in a kind of sedimentation in which only the most recent layers seem to be active justifications for rejection. The others, more deeply concealed, are no longer fashionable in these rationalistic times. The modern city-dweller finds the reason for rejection of the nomad in myths, while the peasant's indignation remains based on alleged petty thefts whose nature (a chicken or an apple) means more than the monetary loss.

But despite everything, local authorities faced a new policy in the mid-1970s. Although expulsion still occurs, it is increasingly accompanied by confinement and isolation: with central government issuing regulations and the populace clamouring for action, the 'problem' of nomads and Gypsies is solved by enclosing them on a specially designated site. After nearly six centuries of Gypsy presence, it has become obvious that systematic expulsion is pointless: if one state drives Gypsies out, the neighbouring country follows suit and the cycle never ends. Instead, 'reception' sites were suggested, hidden several miles from a main road, in the middle of abandoned fields, behind the cemetery or the rubbish dump. The sites were devoid of facilities, even lacking water. (The nomads were thought to be dirty anyway.) Once driven to such sites, their inhabitants' conditions are unlikely to improve their image. Local newspapers describe and photograph them in mud and filth.

Towns and counties often benefit by opening a site, although in most countries it is only in the 1980s that local authorities seem to have realized this. The gains are both economic and psychological. In Britain it has been noted that it often costs as much to evict nomads (by using Land Rovers to tow their caravans away), and to dig trenches around open spaces to prevent them from settling there, as it does to set up a modest stopping-place. Similarly, the French authorities have found that wire fences, trenches, and metallic signs eat up considerable chunks of local budgets and, unlike the expenses of provisioning a site, they are not eligible for grant support—not to mention the high cost of repeated police action to remove all those who stop illegally.

The psychological gains come in various ways. The provision of campsites and the stated reasons for it blend well with the humanist current that has developed since 1950. The town councillors exult, and the press echoes flattery: 'The town of Quimper is to welcome travellers humanely', though it's no more than a visit to the location of a future campsite (*Ouest-France*, 4 November 1977). The municipal bulletin of Lille speaks of a 'meritorious decision', in 1974, to designate an unequipped site that would be functional some ten years later. Mere compliance with the law, which requires the provision of sites for passing nomads, thus becomes low-cost humanism, and local authorities and the public pick up two big advantages as well: the opening of a site, no matter how small, makes it possible to prohibit camping anywhere else, and the provisions associated with the site—like nurseries and socio-educational activities—facilitate police control.

Some Gypsies have complained that the campsites are no more than 'traps that allow the police to keep an eye on us and arrest us whenever they want' (communiqué sent to the press in January 1977 by 'a group of Manuš in the Val d'Oise', published by the French daily newspaper *Libération*). The design of most sites lends credence to the charge: an entrance alongside the guard's house and a row of rectangles about 5 × 10 yards. The social centre is sometimes located right in the middle, from where everything in the campsite can be seen. Site users are not allowed to organize the use of space themselves. Instead of being prohibited in certain specified areas, camping is now prohibited everywhere except in supervised areas.

The socio-educational trappings make the prohibition look more human and incidentally turn the previously exotic marginal into an ordinary deviant. The campsites become areas of confinement, tiny reservations from which to oversee the freedom of movement of 'persons of nomadic origin'. Why drive the Indians out when the public can have its own tame Indians nearby, to visit now and then? Sympathetic and businesslike councils may permit stalls to be set up—after all, there may be some tax revenue. Some campsites are purgatories to prepare Gypsies for the paradise of a proper concrete house. Some are called transit sites: temporary cities for recalcitrant nomads who cannot get used to walls.

Rejection of the nomad is one of the views most widely shared by the settled populace and the local authorities. The rejection is bound up with the public's image of nomads and Gypsies, virtually unchanged for centuries. What varies, in the way policy is explained, are the reasons given to justify the treatment of Gypsies and nomads. The traditional fear of brigandage has eased, but still crops up in a masked and mythical form. The Gypsy who shows up in some town is still both strange and alien, a 'vagrant'. Gypsies have no fixed address or residence, their origin is unknown, and they are accused of concealing their real identity, changing their role according to circumstance, and disturbing public order and sanitation. Since they have no home country, Gypsies cannot be understood by the usual indicators. Central governments view them as potential dissidents whose very existence may threaten public order, while for the populace and the local authorities they reactivate fantasies that trouble the community's psychological equilibrium. The elusive nomad must be made ordinary, placed on an official site to be dealt with by the welfare bureaucracy in the normal way. It is not a new idea. At various times in history only the officially recognized

Roadside stop in Kent, 1978

No return: the same site a week later

poor were helped by the community, while foreign vagabonds were expelled or incarcerated [109, quoted by 24, p. 352].

Sometimes Gypsies become a political football, kicked back and forth between different local authorities and various layers of government. The police say the nomads are a local-government problem, town and county councils call them a national problem but then prove reluctant to implement minis-terial recommendations. Mayors consider the nomads a matter for state policy; for the state they are a matter for the mayors.

In effect, in most questions involving Gypsies and nomads, local authorities act as a buffer between central government, whose policy since the middle of the twentieth century has been one of assimilation, and the local populace who have remained rejectionist. Since the 1970s regional authorities have generally fallen in with central government positions and have asked the mayors and local councils to set up campsites. The local authori-ties are therefore gradually becoming links in a chain instead of buffers. Policies are becoming more uniform. Since 1980 the rejection advocated by some and the assimilation pressed by others have become differences of form rather than susbtance. All now seem to agree on the final solution: every nomadic family must find its place on a lot in an approved site; the families whose occupations depend on mobility will have to be supported by social security while a process of cultural assimi-lation unfolds. Rejection of the nomad will then end (since there will be no more nomads to reject), only to reappear in other forms of social segregation.

Stereotypes and Prejudices

The prejudicial and stereotyped images of Gypsies current among non-Gypsies are vitally important, for they go a long way in determining and justifying attitudes to Gypsies and how they are treated. Since the fifteenth and sixteenth centuries, when town chroniclers and lawmakers began issuing descriptions of Gypsies, a whole imagery has been built up, often crystallized in the form of crude stereotypes. An arsenal of names and adjec-tives is now available, on which everyone can draw, depending on the goal and circumstances—the rejectionist mayor, the pro-assimilation legislator, the well-intentioned social worker. The image serves to rationalize the measures taken and the measures in turn fuel the image, thus reinforcing it. Certain individuals are Gypsies and are therefore banished. The juxtaposition of terms then turns into a cause-and-effect relation: once banished, they remain subject to expulsion, and banishment becomes part of the definition of Gypsy.

More recently, when the aim is not to banish but to assimilate, the language shifts in a different direction, and use of the image becomes a kind of ethnocide in advance: Gypsies are deprived of their cultural qualities and become 'persons of nomadic origin' for whom nomadism is no more than an attribute (in any case inaccurate for some Gypsies) ascribed to a distant and no longer relevant origin. These Gypsies—now deprived, by this description, of roots and identity—then represent a 'social problem' of 're-adaptation' that must be solved in order to absorb them into the rest of society. Once defined as targets of readaptation, they are 'objectively' perceived as ill-adapted and their lack of adaptation then becomes part of their image in non-Gypsy eyes. Gypsies are not defined as they really are, but as socio-political requirements say they have to be.

The various images of Gypsies are actually revealing of non-Gypsies, whose reaction is typically ambivalent, a combination of attraction and repulsion. For sedentary people, nomadism, whether real or imagined, is dangerous and perverse, a threat to the stability of civilization. If for Gypsies nomadism symbolizes a lack of attachment to places and events, for non-Gypsies it is also a symbol, indeed the very basis of their rejection. Gypsies live from day to day, and in the West that happens to be synonymous with improvidence, a great defect. The ants have always criticized the grasshoppers, but have always envied them too. Whether as beggar princes or princely beggars, the Gypsies, with their weird music and dance, serve as public opinion's scapegoat, all the more angrily rejected exactly because they are attractive, all the more strictly prohibited because they are so elusive, leading an exasperatingly ambiguous life on the margins of society.

I don't know what goes on in the gadžo's head. One thing

for sure, when he looks at us he feels that he's seeing something very important, an independence, a way of . . . The thing is, most of the time, he says that the women are pretty, that they dance well, that Gypsies are good musicians . . . I mean, you have this feeling that he thinks Gypsies are great, while you know he's saying to himself . . . Which explains why in order to reject them, he has to resort to all that dirty stuff, you know, like that we carry lice, we're filthy, we don't work, our children do whatever they want . . . Well, it's not easy to figure out what the gadžo really means. Deep down, he's rejecting something he finds very nice, but unattainable—it's unattainable, so he rejects it. And if he acts really nasty, it's because he's angry. At the same time, though, it's not that simple; if you ask a gadžo, he wouldn't say anything like that. But that's how *I* feel about it. Because where they used to cut out your tongue if any of us spoke Romany, I know that in the local school they called me lice-ridden, but when I was 14, at high school, it was 'Oh, you're a Gypsy, that's really neat, I wish I was too,' and so on. It's these two things at the same time, you know? [11].

It was especially easy for false images to arise, because there was no convenient category in which to place the Gypsies. And since no one was in a position to counter them, stereotypes quickly became accepted. When Gypsies first arrived in Europe, they were called Egyptians, Saracens, Indians, or even Pagans; sometimes they were simply described without being named, for there were no precedents. They were always associated with others whom they resembled superficially: 'Sorcerers, jugglers, and pickpockets/Vile cast-offs/Of an ancient world/Sorcerers, jugglers, and pickpockets/Carefree Bohemians, whence do you come?' (Béranger). Gypsies figure in pejorative expressions in numerous languages: '*Voleur comme un Bohémien, sale comme un Gitan, vestido como un Gitano, embustero como un Gitano*, to gyp, a gypsy cab driver . . .' But there was always ambiguity too. 'Our lives/They must envy', goes a Gypsy saying. Aristocrats gave them lodgings and watched the women dance. Kings received some at court while sending others to the galleys.

Prejudices and stereotypes have by now found their way into dictionaries, which, just because they are reference works, further establish and extend them. Spelling-books and primers teach them to children from their earliest school-days. (See, for example, D. S. Kenrick, *Portrayal of the Gypsy in English School-books*, Internationale Schulbuchforschung, 1984, 1.) Since virtually the whole school population is affected, the stereotypes are spread far and wide, and reinforced by the press and popular literature, which give us the swarthy Gypsy who steals chickens and the Gypsy Baron of operetta. But dictionaries, schoolbooks, the press, and television soap operas say what their makers think will be best received. In other words, they merely crystallize what is already widespread in public opinion, and their authors draw on the same stock of ideas as the drafters of laws. It is the usual circle of cause and effect: dictionaries, books, and the popular press feed on public opinion, turn bits and pieces of fashionable images into official truths, and then reissue them to a public that finds confirmation of its opinion in the authoritative dictionary and the prestigious press.

Although the stereotypes have changed somewhat over the centuries, the theme of the repulsive nomad is constant—and intermixed with the ambiguous (and sometimes attractive) myth of the Gypsy. The settled population is generally intolerant of contacts and relations with nomads. And the worst nomad is always the one who is close by, the one who is camping on someone's doorstep, or at least liable to do so: the dirty Gypsy, the frightening thief. The further away the nomad is, the better. When Gypsies are so far away that they verge on myth, they suddenly become alluring: handsome, artistic, living un-trammelled lives, symbols of freedom. They are accepted provided they are confined to designated areas and to folklore: music and dance, the circus, caravans in approved sites. The only good Gypsy is the mythical one—the one who does not exist.

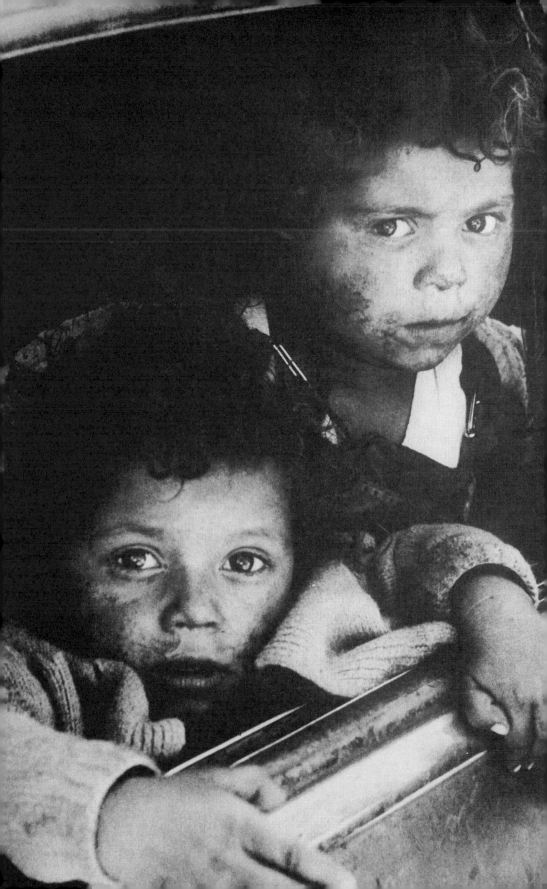

4

CHANGING TIMES

In recent years Gypsies have responded to the pressures of their environment by developing their own organizations, some national, others international.

Gypsy Organizations in the Past

The history of Gypsy organizations is not linear, but the roots of the present groups are deep and diffuse.

Gypsy social organization is not conducive to the emergence of a system based on chiefs or leaders. When they first arrived in Europe, however, Gypsies are reported to have said that they had a king or a queen. The veracity of this report cannot be checked; moreover, it is part of the legends current at the time and embellished by the chroniclers who recorded them. The Gypsies seem to have adapted to prevalent ways of thinking by mimicking the terminology of their environment. In France in the fifteenth century they said they were led by 'counts' or 'dukes' 'of Little Egypt'; in Hungary and Poland they used the words voïvode, vajda, wojt, or vataf; in Scotland they said 'lord'. Later on, in France, their 'chief' was called 'captain', and was assisted by a 'lieutenant'. In the Basque country in the nineteenth century there is even mention of a 'prefect' [133, p. 55]. Gypsy chiefs were sometimes designated by rulers who wanted to deal with an official representative (notably in Poland). These examples from the past may be compared with the present-day 'presidents' and 'secretaries-general' found in most countries.

As for so-called Gypsy kings, they seem not to have suffered

143

the whims of fashion, for there is still talk of them among Gypsies today. In the twentieth century, this myth of kings and queens has become essentially journalistic. It is usually upon the death of a family head that Gypsies, fearful of being expelled from their stopping-place, start a rumour that the deceased was a man of importance, the 'king'. The large number of mourners (who actually assemble for every funeral) and the mixture of fact and fiction supplied to the press give credence to the supposition of a royal corpse. Public opinion is thus shaped in part by a myth started by the Gypsies themselves. That same myth, picked up and embroidered by journalists and their readers, the latter exercising their own imagination, is then beamed back to the Gypsies in various ways: through television, contacts with gadže, and so on. The Gypsies may then endeavour to adapt it, some prominent figure claiming to be a king and demanding a territory over which to rule. Some even have themselves crowned, carry royal insignia, and draw up programmes which, however mythical, inspire others who may seek to implement them.

Once given formal shape and rationalization, the myth becomes a utopia, and it is but a short step from myth-maker to utopian theorist. In the late twenties, in Poland, utopia found fertile soil. Several members of the Kwiek family (from Romania) had themselves officially recognized as Gypsy 'kings', from which designation they derived a number of privileges and a few duties. The police and government endorsed elections of kings. In 1930 Michael Kwiek II succeeded his father, Gregory. He even had a court. During a meeting held in 1934 he declared his desire to assure the happiness of all Gypsies, in particular by creating a state on the banks of the Ganges. Then he organized his election for a further five years but was soon compelled to leave Poland. In a statement issued on 7 February 1935 Mathias Kwiek in turn declared himself king and sent the Polish president some proposals for reforming the life of the Roma. Michael's supporters were still on the scene, however, and prevented Mathias from gaining wide recognition. Joseph Kwiek, who sent an envoy to the League of Nations to ask for some land in South Africa (believing that it would take 'too long' to get a region of Poland), also failed to get elected — as did Basil, an old opponent of Michael. Finally, 4 July 1937 saw the splendiferous coronation of Januš Kwiek. Invitations were sent to heads of state and to members of the diplomatic corps resident in Vienna. Posters were printed and leaflets distributed. The invitations bore the inscription 'Januš Kwiek, president of the candidates to the throne of the Gypsies', accompanied by a stamp and a crown of fleurs-de-lis, although there were actually five candidates.

Thousands of people came to the army stadium in Warsaw, where the election was to be held. The candidates' formal dress had been rented from the Warsaw Opera House: tails, white tie, and top hat. The electors, some thirty 'elders', deposited their ballot papers in a golden urn. The election had to be recognized as official and legal so that Mussolini, who had been asked to provide some land in Abyssinia, would consider the request. Duly elected, Januš was crowned by the archbishop. A salute was fired and Januš then made a speech in Romany. 'To begin with,' he said, 'I will send a delegate to Mussolini asking him to grant us a strip of territory in Abyssinia for the settlement of the Gypsies. Our people have had enough of wandering through the ages. The time has come for us to cease living as nomads. If they allow us to send our children to Polish schools, there to be educated, we shall soon have representatives of our own in the League of Nations.' Subsequently, however, Januš was accused of having bribed the voters in this electoral farce. Then came the war and the German occupation. In 1946 Rudolf Kwiek proclaimed himself king of the Gypsies, but then abandoned that title in favour of 'president of the World Council of Gypsies'. He died in obscurity in 1964, at the age of 87. Some members of the Kwiek family had moved to the Paris region and were among the earliest members of the organization called the World Gypsy Community (CMG) (see pp. 00 ff).

During the same period another more collective form of organization arose in Romania. In 1926 a local association of Roma was formed in Clabor (Fagaras), patterned after the German 'neighbourhood associations'. Between 1930 and 1934 a journal was published, called *Neamul Tiganesc* (The Gypsy Family). In 1933 the General Association of Roma in Romania was founded by a non-Gypsy journalist, Lasurica. This association, which survived for only one year, produced two newspapers, *Glasul Romilor* (The Voice of the Roma), which was distributed

nationally, and *O Rom*, with a smaller circulation. A national
conference was held in Bucharest in 1934 and established the
Uniunea Generala a Romilor din Romania (General Union of Roma
of Romania), which held many meetings up to 1939. It was led
by Gheorghe Nicolescu, a settled Rom who was a flower dealer
in Bucharest and a representative of an intellectual bourgeoisie
of integrationist inclination: he sought to settle the nomads
(whereas the General Association was far more 'nationalist').
Once again, however, the Second World War halted the rise of
Gypsy organizations, and it was almost thirty years before Gypsies dared openly to call themselves Gypsies again (personal
communication from Alexandru Danciu). The only exception
seems to be in Greece, where in 1939 two women belonging to a
Gypsy group that had settled near Athens in 1930 or so set up
the Panhellenic Cultural Association of Greek Gypsies, which is
still active today.

Ionel Rotaru came from Romania. In May 1959, near the race-
track at Enghien-les-Bains, he had himself crowned 'supreme
chief of the Gypsy people' and assumed the name Vajda Voïvod.
He then began issuing a flood of statements to the press and
embarked on various symbolic actions. Myth was his most effective weapon. 'In this Lille hotel,' wrote one journalist, 'I felt that
for the first time in my life I stood before a man of royal blood'
(*La Voix du Nord*, 9 September 1970). Another offered this
account: 'Short, dark, lively, about fifty, alert and with a dig-
nified but wholly unaffected air, Mr Rotaru holds court in
Montreuil-sous-Bois in a two-room flat with kitchen on the
second floor of a building quite incommensurate with the quality
of its tenant' (*La Dépêche de Toulouse*, 23 May 1965). Given
credibility by the press, the myth won him a wide audience, but
Rotaru ultimately remained its prisoner: when he called himself
'supreme chief', the journalists translated the title as 'king', and
later, when he began calling himself 'president', he was stuck
with 'king'. Myth goes down easier than everyday reality, and a
press conference by the king of the Gypsies, by definition
picturesque, has much greater box-offce appeal than the
announcement of a communiqué by a Gypsy bureaucrat issued
after a meeting of the board of directors.

Shortly after his coronation, Rotaru founded two associations, the National Gypsy Organization (ONG), which never attracted much attention, and the CMG, which made a big splash and still exists. The CMG included Rom, Manuš, and Kalé from France and had contacts in Poland (in particular through the Kwieks), Canada, Turkey, and other countries. The aim of the organization was to wage the fight against 'illiteracy, obscurantism, and poverty'. Rotaru stated that he 'had to have offices, a press service, and a cultural department', and that he planned to visit Gypsy communities 'from Mexico to Australia'. In 1962 he asked the people of Lyons to contribute land to make the city the world capital of the Gypsies. Some time later he announced at a press conference that he would ask the United Nations for territory in Somalia. He even provided details about how the new country would be governed.

For about twenty years (he died in early 1982), Rotaru developed his ideas in several directions. He wanted to reduce the suspicion with which Gypsies are regarded, to persuade the young to join vocational centres to learn a trade, to repeal the 1912 law (then still in effect in France), to set up caravan schools, to organize campsites near inhabited areas, to establish an international status for Gypsies, to win reparations for the damage suffered under the Nazi regime, and to publish works in the Gypsy language. In 1964 the CMG sent all French National Assembly deputies a letter in which Rotaru asked the Assembly to consider a bill he had drawn up. The letter concluded: 'If all the money the French government has been allocating to the gypsy problem all these years had been used for these purposes, there would no longer be any Gypsy problem in France.'

In 1964 Rotaru opened a cultural centre in Brussels which lasted for five months. He continually pursued the German authorities to secure payment of war reparations to Gypsies who were entitled to them. But the myth surrounding him kept him a utopian to the end: he had a cabinet, named ministers and deputies, demanded territory, printed Gypsy passports. He also raised money through selling paintings by various masters (Rouault, Mathieu, Picasso, Leonor Fini, Foujita, Balthus) which had been given to him for 'social and cultural efforts' that were not always clearly defined. On 26 February 1965 the govern-

Pentecostal baptism, France ▷

ment issued a decree dissolving the CMG. But as Rotaru told the press six years later, 'dissolution is not prohibition', and he continued to issue statements that captivated journalists.

There were other utopians besides Rotaru, though less ambitious. Utopia, in fact, is not unimportant. It brings the problems of Gypsies to the attention of the gadže, sometimes forces governments to take a stand, and excites public opinion, albeit by drenching itself in myth. Moreover, the Gypsy organizations that did arise were nurtured in this realm of the imagination. Utopia is a transitional phase in a people's self-awakening, and utopian projects, even if they are only faltering creations of an immature organization, become political acts. Finally, utopian projects express the deepest concerns of the people who produce them. The demand for a territory, for instance—often called Romanestan—is undoubtedly the most difficult to achieve, and therefore the most utopian in the strict sense, but it is a sign of an attempt to recover some sense of balance at a time when Gypsies are finding it more and more difficult to maintain their identity. Rotaru spoke of 'a territory that would serve as a refuge in the event of persecution', and the idea of such a territory as a symbolic force is more important than its actual existence [for a detailed discussion of this issue, see 69, the chapter entitled 'L'image de l'utopie'].

In 1965 the CMG lost most of its leadership. A dissident group split from Rotaru and founded the International Gypsy Committee (CIT). Its president was Vanko Rouda, who concentrated on the more realistic of the CMG's goals, in particular the demand for war reparations from Germany. The CIT proposed that the administrative difficulties be handled by paying the money to an international body that would supervise its use. *La Voix Mondiale Tzigane*, the CIT's organ, echoed its policy:

> We seek to be the common denominator of Gypsies throughout the world . . . to bring together all the disparate elements of our people, unnoticed by most but real enough to give them voice and carry it everywhere: that is an important task.

At the conclusion of these days of discussion, a number

of decisions were made which together constitute a plan of action for the months and years ahead:

to strengthen the structure of the various Gypsy bodies through the creation of committees in every town in France with a significant Gypsy community;

to seek new members constantly;

to study the possibilities of purchasing accommodation centres and sites for camping;

to train Gypsy leaders;

to pursue and enhance the information campaign about the Gypsy people, its values, conditions, and needs;

to distribute *La Voix Mondiale Tzigane* to an ever-growing number of Gypsy families.

Although associations to defend Gypsies arose in France and other countries after the second world war, none of these succeeded in giving the Gypsies their due. We faced the paradox that various associations talked about us, even spoke in our name, without having a single Gypsy member. Moreover, we soon discovered that the various bodies dealing with Gypsies were torn by many little internal wars. We then told ourselves that we Gypsies had enough problems without looking for trouble among others and dividing ourselves in all these organizations. That is why we decided to found our own organizations. (Extracts from several issues of *La Voix Mondiale Tzigane*.)

The paper ceased publication in 1968, but others followed. In England the Gypsy Council (see page 00), affiliated to the CIT, published *Romano Drom*, which developed similar ideas:

Pralale Romale, kako si o pervo amare publikatsiako ande Anglia [Brother Rom, this is our first paper in England] . . . We shall not rest until all the world's Gypsies can live in freedom and without fear. Let us work together until we obtain our rights, until our voice is heard in all countries. We are Roma and not dogs, and we have our rights under the Charter of the United Nations. We Roma number close to ten million throughout the world, and we must remember the watchword 'United we stand, divided we fall.' Our strength is our brotherhood. We must work together for a better tomorrow for our children, our families, our people. We Roma have rights, the right to live according to our laws and customs. Not so long ago half a million of us died in concentration camps. These Roma died for freedom. We who are alive today now want our freedom, the freedom to live in peace, without oppression. (Ronald Lee, *Romano Drom*, no. 1, June 1969.)

Katarina Taikon wrote in *Zigenaren*, the journal of the Gypsies in Sweden:

The idea that we would like to become 'Swedes' like you is one of the most common misunderstandings. We do not want to become like 'you'. We simply want to be rid at last of your prejudices and restrictions, which prevent us from living freely. Becoming like 'you' seems to me quite unhealthy. Swedish culture and civilization have not attained any definitive ideal whatsoever: many currently accepted ways of life and thinking are terribly base and are anything but models to be aped. And why should we be content to ape them? To become like 'you' would be categorically to devalue 'us' [116].

Matéo Maximoff, a Rom writer in France, said at a meeting of the CIT in Freiburg in 1972: 'We do not wish to revolt, but nor do we wish to be oppressed.' Juan de Dios Ramírez Heredia, a Kalé and member of the Spanish parliament, expressed similar thoughts:

We want to be the architects of our own destiny . . . We have no illusion that we can fight the Goliath symbolized by a powerful technocratic society when we are so few in number, so poor, and so inadequately trained to fight with the same weapons. In this we may contemplate the words of Azorín: 'I then understood that trying to make the revolution when you lack the means is like pissing against the walls of the Bank of Spain.' We are now concerned with

Distribution of gold coins before death ▷

two clearly defined aims: first, to gain recognition of our dignity as human beings and due respect for our indigenous culture; second, to secure better living conditions so that many of our brothers still living in poverty and indigence can rise from them ... The promotion of an entire people is what is at issue ... [a people] who, among its most cherished values, feels enormous pride in being Gypsy, which means that beyond the sufferings, vicissitudes, and persecutions, the spirit of a people, of a distinct and different group, motivates us and will continue to motivate us ... so that we continue to be, above all else, Gypsies [97, pp. 204, 208, 218].

The CIT soon became a kind of federation linking various national organizations (a total of twenty-three as of 1972, representing groups from twenty-two countries). New groups sprang up in more and more countries, often with CIT assistance, and the network became quite extensive, with a presence in Greece, Finland, Czechoslovakia (the Cultural Union of Roma of Slovakia and the Union of Roma of the Czech Republic, both of which, however, were dissolved by the government soon after), and Yugoslavia, where Abdi Faik, the president of *Romano Pralipe*, was a member of parliament in Macedonia. Another association, in Belgrade, was led by the writer Slobodan Berberski. In December 1966 Gypsies gathered by Vanko Rouda and Grattan Puxon (who had previously founded a Traveller organization in Ireland) met in a pub in Kent with a 'No Gypsies' sign hanging outside and founded the Gypsy Council. In the following years, this organization was active in helping Gypsies to resist police evictions and played a vital role in the rise of awareness of Gypsies among the authorities and public opinion in Britain.

The National Gypsy Education Council was set up in 1970, and in 1975 the Association of Gypsy organizations brought together several groups. The National Association of Gypsies of France was founded in 1962, and the National Committee of Travellers in 1972. Several other organizations were subsequently established in France: the Gypsy Bureau in 1973, the Union of Gypsies and Travellers in France in 1980, the Gypsy

Federation of France in 1981. In Finland, the Association of Gypsies of Finland was founded in 1967; in Sweden, the Association of Finnish Gypsies in Stockholm was established in 1972 and was followed by the creation of a dozen other associations; the two organizations mentioned, later joined by others, formed the Nordic Rom Council in 1973. In West Germany the Association of Sinti in Germany was established in 1952; it later became the German Sinti League and still exists today. In 1982, following an agreement among several regional organizations, a national body was founded (the Central Council of Sinti and Roma) which now has a corresponding association in each state of West Germany. Other organizations have continued to develop in other countries: the Association of Travellers in Switzerland (1974), the National Gypsy Committee in Italy (1978), the Irish Traveller Community in Ireland (1962), and the Committee for the Rights of Travellers (1981) and *Minceir Misli* (1984), these last two also in Ireland.

Opré Roma!

The CIT organized the First World Romany Congress in London from 8 to 12 April 1971. The delegates rejected the terms Gypsy, Tsigane, Zigeuner, and Gitano, which were not their own and did not reflect reality, adopting instead the term Rom. The CIT (International Gypsy Committee) was renamed the International Rom Committee, or in Romany *Komiteto Lumniako Romano* (KLR), and Vanko Rouda was confirmed as president [for details, see 69]. The congress was chaired by Slobodan Berberski, who had been elected by the delegates, representing fourteen countries; there were also observers from other countries. Berberski's speech reflected the mood of the congress:

> The goal of this congress is to unite Roma throughout the world and move them to action; to bring about emancipation as we see it and according to our own ideals; to advance at our own speed. There is much to discuss and much to do, and we cannot yet say what methods we will use or what direction we will take. But whatever we do will

be marked by our own particular personality: it will be *amaro Romano drom*, our Romany road.

What we have to fight is exemplified by bureaucracy. Officialdom, now overgrown in every state, is a monster whose job is to squeeze out human feelings, monopolize decision-making, and stifle initiative—qualities which are the very essence of our being. The administrative machine, concerned with standardization and control, by its nature cannot understand that national consciousness—the collective desire to be ourselves—is the well-spring that alone can refresh and renew the world.

Our struggle, to endure according to our own genius, is the same struggle for liberation being waged all over the globe, to prevent continents from being turned into deserts by war, expropriation and misgovernment.

Our people must combine and organize to work locally, nationally, and internationally. Our problems are the same everywhere: we must proceed with our own forms of education, preserve and develop our Romany culture, bring a new dynamism into our communities, and forge a future in accordance with our life-style and beliefs. We have been passive long enough, and I believe—starting today—we can succeed.

In a marked spirit of unity, it was proclaimed that, *Sa o Roma phrala* (All Roma are brothers). They had the same aspirations in various countries; several organizations had been able to come together, and the Roma were discovering one another at the same time as they were being discovered by others. The KLR, a federation of national committees, became the permanent secretariat and executive body of the congress, which was the supreme authority, the 'parliament'. A flag and an anthem were adopted. Five commissions were established: social affairs; education; war crimes (research on genocide under the Nazis, preparation of files documenting war crimes); language (to ensure preservation and development of Romany, and standardization to facilitate exchanges and publications); and culture. The congress was summed up in a single slogan: *O narodo Romano si les derečo te arakhel pesko drom karig o progreso* (The Rom people has the right to seek its own road to progress).

Delegates left in a confident mood, determined to bring about unity in their local areas. New committees arose in several countries. The KLR continued its co-ordination efforts and stepped up contacts with international bodies, especially the Council of Europe.

The Second World Romany Congress was held from 8 to 11 April 1978 in Geneva. It was attended by some sixty delegates and an equal number of observers from twenty-six countries. The second congress was in no way a mere repetition or amplification of the first. To begin with, it was marked by mutual recognition between the Roma and India: the Roma spoke of their attachment to the 'mother country', and India powerfully underscored its attachment to its 'children', sending several delegates as well as messages from the minister of foreign affairs, the minister of education and social affairs, and the prime minister of the Punjab. India also expressed support for Gypsy demands at the United Nations.

The second congress, unlike the first, was marked by sharp disputes and differences. Outsiders who had not followed the Gypsy organizations considered these differences evidence of confusion and disunity, and the befuddled 'special envoys' of the press complained that it was impossible to figure out how the various Romany committees worked, as if the internal workings of Romany committees ought to follow the model of non-Gypsy bodies. But although the antagonisms made it impossible to present a united front to the authorities or the press, they were evidence that a variety of opinions were being expressed. The congress's wide-ranging action programme sought recognition of the Roma's specific culture and their right to preserve and develop it. The possibility of gaining recognition as a minority of Indian origin was particularly important for all Roma living in the East bloc countries. Recognition by international bodies, the struggle against policies of rejection and assimilation, continuing attempts to standardize the language, and insistence on the request for war reparations from Germany—these were the keynotes of the congress.

The congress was chaired by Jan Cibula. A collegial presidium emerged from the congress, including twelve members:

Musical traditions

159

Menyhert Lakatos (Hungary), Shaip Jusuf (Yugoslavia), W. R. Rishi (India), Jan Cibula (Switzerland), Juan de Dios Ramírez Heredia (Spain), John Tene (US), Sait Balič (Yugoslavia), Stefan Kwiek (Sweden), Grattan Puxon (Greece), Agnes Vranckx (Belgium), Ranjit Naik (India), and Raja Chibb (Pakistan). In addition, a central committee included members from each country. The members of the various commissions were elected, as were delegates to the United Nations, the UN Human Rights Commission, and UNESCO. Neither the Romany nor the (slightly different) English version of the official congress minutes refer to a new organization, although in the discussions the KLR was referred to primarily in the past tense. This was probably because the KLR, organizational power base of Vanko Rouda, opposed the World Romany Congress between 1978 and 1981, when a reconciliation took place. An organization to carry on the work of the congress before its next meeting was, however, established. It has sometimes been called the *Romano International Jekhethanibe* (Romany International Union), and sometimes the *Romano Ekhipe* (Romany Union). Under the latter name, it was granted consultative status at the UN Social and Economic Commission in 1979, thus achieving a key point in the congress's programme.

The Third World Romany Congress was held from 16 to 20 May 1981 at Göttingen, Germany, at the invitation of the German Sinti League and with the support of the Association for Threatened Peoples. This time it was attended by some three hundred delegates from twenty-two countries, including Australia, Belgium, Britain, Bulgaria, Denmark, Finland, France, Greece, Hungary, India, Ireland, the Netherlands, Norway, Pakistan, Poland, Romania, Spain, Sweden, Switzerland, the United States, West Germany, and Yugoslavia. The Italian and Czech delegations had travel problems. This congress, the first held on German soil, was dominated by the fate of Gypsies under the Nazi regime. Survivors of concentration camps told of their experiences, the German organizations recalled their many attempts to win reparations, and the congress renewed, in stronger terms than ever, its call for a general settlement of this issue. New elections to the presidium were held, and the body was enlarged by a decision that one member

Travelling circus, France

from each national state should be represented on it. Sait Balič
(Yugoslavia) was now president of the presidium, Romani Rose
(Germany) was vice-president, and Rajko Djurič (Yugoslavia)
was secretary.

It emerged at this congress that unity was still a difficult
proposition, for many reasons. But everyone felt that the world
organization was gaining strength, and, as the final resolution
stated: 'The congress is a great step on the road to the unity of
the Romany people' [see a selection of press articles on the
congress in 102]. *Opré Roma!* — Roma arise! That slogan has
become ever more widespread since the 1971 congress.

The rise of Gypsy organizations has encouraged Gypsies to
speak out, to seek recognition and respect, to have the world
take notice of them. In 1979, when the United Nations gave
consultative status to the Romany Union, representing seventy-

one associations in twenty-one countries, it was seen as endorsement and encouragement, an essential step towards world recognition. Gypsies began speaking out in many different ways, all of them new, since until then Gypsies had had to be as inconspicuous as possible in order to overcome obstacles without suffering too much harm.

Press statements and protests against certain abuses were issued. Official statements were made when the opportunity arose, and Gypsies began taking the floor to voice their criticism and opposition at official meetings. Their voices were especially sharp for having been so long suppressed. Gypsies began using the radio, something that will probably intensify. They turned to the press. Organizations presented motions to various ministries, with demands and proposals relating to the situation of the Gypsies. And—something very new for such a fundamentally nomadic people who tended not to dwell on the past—monuments and plaques were placed to commemorate the massacre of Gypsies under the Nazi regime. There is one in the camp at Bergen-Belsen. Its inscription reads:

> *In deep sadness*
> *and with profound respect*
> *we, Sinti, remember*
> *the victims of our people.*
> *Through their violent death*
> *they exhort the living to resist*
> *the injustices committed*
> *by man against man.*

Resistance has recently taken a form little known among Gypsies before 1980: demonstrations, quite the opposite of the previous deliberate attempts to be inconspicuous. On 26 March 1980, for example, a demonstration was held at the West German Embassy in Paris demanding war reparations and asking that a procedure for the re-examination of wartime cases be established. In April of that year a hunger strike was organized in support of the same demand. It lasted eight days, was covered by about a hundred journalists and television reporters, and had considerable impact.

Gypsy Power

Broadly speaking, we can distinguish three periods in the development of Gypsy organization. The 1960s saw a trend towards the formation of organized groups, the London Congress (1971) confirming their existence and their international ties. In the 1970s these organizations took root, although the Geneva Congress (1978) revealed the divisions among them. The 1980s have seen the organizations achieve a certain stability, the Göttingen Congress (1981) marking the first phase of that process. The international extension of meetings, the study of problems, and the putting forward of demands have also been features of the 1980s: the Yugoslav influence at Göttingen, the fact that the president and secretary are both Yugoslav Roma, the participation of delegates from India and Pakistan, and of more delegates from the United States put an end to the West European bias that had previously been so evident.

Things have changed fast, but that was inevitable, for there have been major and equally rapid changes in other societies. Gypsies had long been trapped between the allure of a myth (handsome, artistic, unrestrained, but consigned to folkore) and the wretched stereotype of the nomad (dirty, a thief and always too close for comfort). So pervasive was the image that Gypsies had little choice but to let others see what they expected to see. That was both safer and less costly in psychological terms. It was easier to pretend to conform to what others expected than to try to fight back. The struggle would have been too one-sided and its target—prejudice—was too intangible and elusive, multifarious and tenacious. But pretence only fuelled what it sought to evade, and the image was further consolidated, Gypsy behaviour simultaneously being determined by it. The vicious circle was not easily broken. Gypsies are both accomplices and victims of the image they have been saddled with, but for centuries they had had no choice but to be its accomplices in order not to be merely its victims. Long experience has taught Gypsies to modulate their behaviour depending on the impact it might have on others. The list of techniques is endless, for they have always been an essential part of the Gypsies' adapt-and-survive life-style.

What has changed in recent years is the complicity: no longer active, it has become passive, like the resistance of which it is the expression. State policies of rejection enabled the Gypsy minority to withdraw. Corporal punishment never broke their spirit. But the policy of assimilation—its application sweeping, its ideology grasping—reaches out to the entire Gypsy population, body and soul. Withdrawal is no longer possible, nor is active resistance. The web of regulations that took shape in the 1970s epitomizes the new order, rigid in its scope, bolstered by complex laws, backed up by social work and social control. Not even coexistence is possible any more, and to be different is acceptable only as folklore. The margins are being erased, and the marginal life faces extinction.

There was no middle way between the policies of rejection and assimilation, any more than there is any happy medium between the myth of the handsome Gypsy and the ominous nomad, or between the expulsion in olden days of the Bohemian whose culture was recognized but rejected and the forced incorporation of today's nomad whose culture is denied while devoured.

Gypsies have been disoriented. Their techniques of adaptation, previously active, are now also becoming passive. Increasingly they suffer what others make them suffer, while their culture, cast adrift, is moored to ever smaller geographical and social units. Their world was once potentially the globe, but now it has become the shanty-town or designated campsite. Once they lived in groups enlarged by marriages and other family alliances, but now they cling tighter day by day to a shrunken family uprooted from its culture to be rooted in one place.

It is against this background that the rise of Gypsy organizations must be seen. 'We believe that we exist. We wonder whether this is not a hallucination. Our only defence against forced assimilation is voluntary seclusion and isolation,' one Hungarian Rom wrote in a letter to a meeting of the KLR in Freiburg in April 1972. Assimilation or dissimulation: that was the alternative. For centuries Gypsies had to disguise themselves in order to appear to blend in. The advent of Gypsy power breaks that alternative and shatters the stereotype of the Gypsy mired for ever in his supposed primitiveness. In a number of countries Gypsies have shaken off their traditional reserve and have sought direct contact with the authorities. They are no longer content to accept the living conditions others prescribe for them and they no longer wish to deal with intermediaries, whether social workers or members of 'associations to assist travelling people'. They have come to realize that the translation of their demands is often a betrayal of their wishes and that the rise of Gypsy organizations enables them to assert their own rights. Intermediaries deal with problems piecemeal, which makes them appear minor. They make the Gypsies seem deviants within the surrounding society, rather than members of a minority with its own demands and a desire for identity. Both nationally and internationally, Gypsy organization represents a rediscovery of community spirit, a reassuring symbol at a time of intense, profound, and recurrent upheavals.

The new Gypsy organizations encountered established orders of two sorts: Gypsy tradition and traditional social organization on the one hand and the non-Gypsy authorities on the other, quite happy to do without the activities and demands of these pressure groups.

On the side of tradition, the fragmented Gypsy order does little to encourage unity. No man can claim authority over another man, no family over another family, no kinship group over another. The Gypsies constitute a mosaic of diversified groups, and although cohesion is possible, unity is not within easy reach. But the new organizations speak in terms of a single Gypsy or Romany entity inconceivable in the logic of social organization. How is unity in an all-embracing movement possible, when emphasis on difference and distinction has been the deep and enduring concern of all Gypsies? 'We must break down internal rivalries and hierarchies,' declared Jan Cibula, president of the Romany Union, in his speech at Bergen-Belsen on 27 October 1979.

The new way of thinking faced particularly severe obstacles in that it challenged the spirit and style of the people and their culture. Gypsy identity had always been a matter of experience more than anything else. In the new organizations, it had to be contemplated, described, questioned. The Gypsies, now pres-

sured by others to demonstrate what it is that sets them apart, must work that distinction out at the risk of congealing it. So they re-examine their past, which had never concerned them, raise monuments to their persecuted dead, and unite behind the demand for war reparations. What the congresses and meetings lose in warmth, they gain in effectiveness. They enter history, from whose vicissitudes they had always felt apart. They find themselves caught up in a political dynamic that involves others as well as themselves. Whereas previously they always sought to live outside geographical limits, they now find themselves hemmed in by government permits when they try to establish organizations. Sometimes they give public praise, whether this is spontaneous or opportunism—to those who seem to allow them to exist and express themselves, giving them visas and sometimes subsidies to attend congresses.

The Gypsies face a fundamental dilemma: to remain Gypsy in the face of the new policy of assimilation, they must organize; but organizing to deal with non-Gypsies means learning to use their tools (such as associations with presidents, treasurers, secretaries, and so on), which in turn means accepting values and ways of doing things that modify life-styles. These come to resemble those of non-Gypsies, which is just what the Gypsies are seeking to avoid. The organized Gypsy, now in a position to respond to the non-Gypsy, looks around to find that tradition has been left behind. Gypsies are acting *gadžikanes*, or like gadže. It is thus understandable that not all Gypsies have rushed to support the presidents and secretaries, who nevertheless are vitally important for the future of *all* Gypsy society. These presidents, secretaries, or leaders have a difficult role to play: too innovative for some Gypsies, not innovative enough for others, and not always in accord with their counterparts in other organizations.

To non-Gypsies, the emergence of Gypsy organizations is disturbing. It is never pleasant to see individuals rise up to defend a culture whose very existence is denied or its extinction sought. The element of denial in political attitudes towards Gypsy populations takes two complementary directions.

On the one hand, the basic features and the dynamism of the culture are minimized, and often cast in a pejorative light (the

◁ On the road, Spain

Gypsies have no land of their own, their language is broken up into dialects, their occupations are not 'vocations', their group consciousness is slight, and their unity a chimera). They are then considered to have no 'real culture'. The culture is undermined by an analysis based on misinterpretation; particular cultural features are taken in isolation, and the larger picture is thus distorted.

On the other hand, the manner in which these populations adapt to the powerful pressures to which they are subjected may be exaggerated. This view tends to mistake the effects of the Gypsies' difficult conditions for remnants of a culture. The protective shell is mistaken for what it is protecting, on the assumption that there is nothing underneath. The result is a perfect justification for the 'readaptation' proposed to or imposed on these individuals, and Gypsy organizations are portrayed as the utopian creations of a handful of misguided activists.

When Gypsy organizations give unimpeachable evidence of their existence (when they are recognized and mentioned by international bodies, for example) two new arguments are advanced. The first, very much humanist in inspiration, suggests that the Gypsy organizations 'preserve the present isolation and separation of Gypsies from the rest of the population, impede all progress proposed to the Gypsies by our environment, and permit preservation of the old primitive Gypsy way of life, with all its negative features'. Such was the official line developed in the 1960s in Czechoslovakia [reported in 51, p. 221]. This argument is designed to justify the banning of Gypsy organizations in the name of progress.

The second argument fastens on a few superficial characteristics of Gypsy organizations to claim that the Gypsy tradition has vanished. The sight of Gypsies wearing ties and glasses and carrying attaché cases is enough to remove all doubts, so there is no point in dwelling on any alleged cultural specificity, which the people using this argument have always denied anyway. This attitude is based on the stereotype of a Gypsy who can hold meetings only sitting round a fire, barefoot and bare-chested. It also ignores the remarkable capacity for adaptation and change that Gypsies have demonstrated over the centuries. Gypsies, like

Janus, have always had to have two faces, one for their own people, the other for the gadže. For the moment, Gypsy organizations are using their face for the gadže: Gypsy power is not directed at Gypsies, but is a defensive weapon against the gadže. Tradition had been unable to act as an effective barrier against the new policies of assimilation. The old tactics of adaptation were not working, and something new was therefore called for.

Changing Times

Opré Roma! The slogan marks the end of an era. Roma arise! In other words: down with invisibility, stand up publicly and be seen by others. The change affects even what used to be folklore. Gypsies, once accomplices in the stereotypes of music and dance, now insist on breaking from it. What used to be no more than an implicit strain in the *cante jondo* of the Kalé or the lament of the Roma from Russia is now becoming explicit struggle, while preserving its quality, for example in the songs of Duo Z (Z as in Zigeuner: Gypsy) in Germany, or the flamenco shows of Mario Maya (*camelamos naquerar*—Kaló for 'we want to speak'), or in the songs and music of Jarko Jovanovič, who was cultural secretary of the International Committee and composer of the international anthem *Gelem Gelem.* If the output of poets is an expression of the consciousness of the people among whom they live, then deep changes are under way among the Gypsies, and the rise of organization is but one indicator and form of those changes. But where the member of an organization is still a Janus with two faces, the artist or poet has but one, and speaks to Gypsies and others alike. This is itself a break with tradition, an end to 'pretending', and in a sense represents some confidence in the gadže, who are now privy to authenticity. The vicious circle of stereotype is broken, and the hope is that the gadžo will understand.

The changes now under way go deep. Not the least of them is that for reasons to do with survival, the various Gypsy and Traveller groups are tending to merge into a single political whole, despite the traditional fragmentation of the Gypsy universe. Change may well be rapid as well as deep, for Gypsies have centuries of experience in adaptation and imitation. They have preserved their independence, and have not been herded into reservations (even slavery in Romania has left few traces, and other attempts at enclosure have failed). In that sense, their struggle need not be resumed, for it has never really ceased. In recent years, the movement has been shaped by a rising trans-nationalism in world politics more generally, one sign of which is the large number of Non-Governmental International Organizations recognized by the United Nations. The UN's recognition of the Romany Union in 1979 encouraged the formation of many other associations and generated greater awareness. The Roma in the United States feel that they have halted the trend of growing isolation; in Serbia and Macedonia there are some thirty socio-cultural organizations; almost every town in Germany has seen the re-emergence of a Romany or Sinti organization in the past several years. In many countries the militancy and persistence of some Gypsy groups trying to establish themselves have led by a kind of osmosis to advance by other, perhaps more cautious and opportunistic groups. This has also persuaded some governments fearful of the first sort to accept the second, thus seeming to take account of the Gypsies' existence.

The ongoing changes seem not to be merely the latest in a long line of Gypsy adaptations. But what, then, is happening? Is organization for self-defence just another step towards assimilation? Will the Gypsies, once plunging headlong into history, look back to discover that they have left their tradition behind? That borrowing the weapons of self-defence and the tools of advancement from others has made them just like these others? To answer in the affirmative would be to reckon without the Gypsies' time-honoured capacity for adaptation. Other peoples have faced similar choices:

> If tradition is deprived of its sacred trappings, it soon becomes apparent that the choice is not between its pious and necessary preservation or its sacrilegious abandonment . . . the idea that the prime concern of Africans in their everyday life is to protect their traditions, even if they

have to ring them with barricades and mount frantic guards, is a white myth, a colonizer's myth. Africans live in a rich reality in which tradition is but one factor among others. Like all other peoples, their attitude to their traditions changes with the endlessly shifting exigencies of adaptation . . . It is typical of a tradition that it must die, whether a violent or natural death, and give way to a new tradition [142].

The Gypsy-power movement now taking root will enable Gypsies to ensure that this new tradition is not imposed on them by the non-Gypsies among whom they live. It is to be hoped that, once the anxiety now attached to it is eased, the main question facing the Gypsies will long remain: *Kai žas ame, Romale?* (Roma, where are we headed?).

5

THE TWILIGHT OF
THE GYPSIES?

Many anthropologists, surprised and delighted to note the stability and tenacity of Gypsy society, seem certain that this society still has a bright future. Granted, the disappearance of the Gypsies has been predicted more than once, yet they have always survived. And admittedly, the Gypsies have so far represented a group 'the study of which shows that history grants even the most deprived the means of survival when the rational evolutionary view that often governs our analyses would suggest that they have no chance at all' [7, p. 13]. The Gypsies themselves, of course, make much of their survival. But claiming to be eternal and seeking to prove it is itself an indication of concern about survival, and may well be a sign of weakness. The constant claim to be a powerful tradition and the insistence on clinging to it actually mask disarray and temper anxiety. Tradition becomes ritual and loses its dynamism. Once the basis of an identity and life-style, it becomes a fortified bunker. Contrary to the stereotype, the most 'traditionalist' are not necessarily the most 'authentic'; often they are simply unable to adapt, and since they cannot advance, they tread water purely in an effort not to go under.

Times have changed. Gypsy strategies of adaptation are threadbare. Their ability to make use of their environment is nearing its limits. Whereas Gypsies once stood *outside* the societies with which they dealt, they are increasingly becoming part of them, and in this new situation they are no longer perceived as simply different, but as opponents, as marginal elements disturbing the social order or as deviants deliberately seeking to live outside it.

◁ Gypsy quarter in Granada

The effects of state policy are compounded by the changes generally affecting societies in the late twentieth century. The generation gap undermines social cohesion and disrupts the sense of community that is so essential to the survival of Gypsy society; television introduces alluring and disturbing cultural models into most homes; rising delinquency, itself a reflection of the tensions at work in society, engenders new mechanisms of social control and helps to legitimize them; economic changes have led to stigmatizing those who lack jobs that are prized by the ideology of the times, and in mass-consumer societies, poverty is the mother of all vices; urbanization restricts camping and therefore travelling, and regulations are plugging up the holes that once made it possible to move around. Until recently, if Gypsies found it necessary to settle down in one place, it was because they were sick or had temporary business problems. But now settlement is becoming the rule.

The present era is crucial. The introduction of assimilationist policies since the early 1960s has tightened the pressure on the Gypsies. Humanist rhetoric may mask what is really happening, but it does not modify the destructive effects. Although the relevant laws are not explicitly directed at Gypsies or Travellers (the words are rarely mentioned in regulations), the restrictions on door-to-door hawking, the camping of caravans, scrap-metal dealing, and so on are mutually reinforcing in their negative effects: when the caravan loses its wheels, its owners lose their source of income dynamism, and their ability to adapt. The tissue of relations that give individuals their identity is torn. Where once identity was a source of security, it now becomes a well-spring of conflict. The culturally destroyed, socially passive, psychologically unstable, and physically disturbed individuals then find themselves supervised and dependent—especially financially—on the 'social allowances' granted by the state.

After centuries of repeated failure in their efforts to cast Gypsies out, governments are now pursuing a policy whose effects may well prove irreversible. In many respects, assimilation is not incompatible with continued rejection. Just because they are now wage-earners does not mean that Gypsies will no longer suffer oppression. In Hungary it was thought that integration in jobs, housing, and schooling would reduce prejudice against Gypsies, but long experience has proven this hypothesis false. In Romania, Gypsies number nearly a million, but officially they no longer exist (which may be why in Romania, as in Bulgaria and Czechoslovakia, Gypsy women are frequently sterilized: political desire may thus become social reality). The official line is similar to that of France: there are only 'persons of Gypsy or nomadic origin', 'remnants of the past'. But this does not prevent professionally 'integrated' Gypsies from still being considered Gypsies and suffering discrimination (being paid less than non-Gypsies, for example). Nor does it put a stop to posters warning the public to beware of pickpockets and portraying Gypsies as the malefactors. Nor has it ever stopped the authorities themselves from cultivating pejorative images of Gypsies, from calling them dirty, lazy, violent 'social parasites'. Gypsies are openly named when their appearance is politically useful, or when a scapegoat is needed. Ambiguous terms like 'persons of nomadic origin' in France or 'citizens of Gypsy origin' in Czechoslovakia are functional in their imprecision: they simultaneously assimilate and stigmatize; they deny particularity by consigning it to the past; they describe without naming. They are thus infinitely adaptable.

The policies of counterfeit economic and social integration not only undermine Gypsy culture but also jeopardize the means of existence of nomads and Gypsies.

Gypsy trades traditionally permit constant adaptation to changes in prevailing conditions and allow independence, control of work-time, and itinerancy. Cutting off the sources of revenue, which are also in harmony with the cultural context, is one way of forcing dissident marginals back into the fold or of driving them even further out. First it is noted that Gypsy society is underdeveloped. Experts then endeavour to show, with figures more intuitive than real, that the incomes of Gypsies and nomads are low, that they lack savings and pension provisions. Humanitarians of all hues then classify these poor people as subproletarians who require the uplifting experience of entering the 'world of labour'. And since urbanization and industrialization go hand in hand, the transit site and public housing, or the fenced-in and supervised campsite are proposed as alternatives to open stopping grounds. But when the caravan stops

175

for good, the nomad loses all ability to adapt and faces the impasse erected by the sedentary populace.

Then a narrow escape-hatch is opened, leading to a 'well-kept' fixed caravan or flat, under the supervision of a social worker. A 'regular' job will lead the nomad to rehabilitation in society's eyes. Good behaviour will lead to eligibility for financial assistance, and this aid will lead to occupancy of a cramped flat instead of a caravan. The nomad then becomes a sub-proletarian again. Wage-labour isolates and individualizes. Social and psychological problems are aggravated, and members of the family, parents, grandparents, and collateral relatives, are no longer cared for by the Gypsy community in the same way.

Yet in many ways the economic activities of Gypsies and nomads are well adapted to the society in which they live, and may be even more so in years to come. Certain aspects of Gypsy life, perhaps paradoxically, mirror the aspirations of some members of settled society (more free time, greater self-reliance, more co-operation and 'togetherness', and so on). Experts believe that door-to-door hawking has a promising future; special sites are now provided in commercial centres and pedestrian streets for the rising number of open-air stalls, and it might well be possible 'to make better use of the trades of Travellers in a society which, despite certain appearances, needs them more than is generally believed and more than they believe themselves' [33, pp. 11 and 14].

But the present trend of state policy towards Gypsies offers little hope of proper recognition of their economic activities or of any aid in this regard. The time-honoured hostility to the 'Bohemian' persists, and is expressed at best in a passive sympathy with folklore. Centuries ago, when aristocrats and kings let a few Gypsies into their salons, it was only to dance for their guests' amusement; meanwhile, out on the roads, the other Gypsies were being sent to the galleys. Today, people love Gypsies in films and operettas. Ensconced in their boxes at the theatre, they luxuriate in nostalgia and emotion to the sound of violins. Meanwhile, out on the highway, the flesh-and-blood Gypsy lives in poverty.

It is the Gypsy who suffers the effects of this dichotomy. The Gypsy life is fine as a hobby, and the trailer rented for a summer in the Camargue or Ireland is free to roam the roads. But let the trailer or caravan become a permanent and traditional dwelling, and it is suddenly confined to designated sites. The human and financial costs entailed are high, and the sites are spurned by the very people for whom they are intended, since they are well aware of the limits imposed and the consequences of those limits. The alternative now faced by Gypsies is unpalatable: to stay different is to be considered deviant and to be treated as such; to conform is to blend away through assimilation.

Under the pressure of Gypsy organizations, a few governments have accorded Gypsies the rights enjoyed by officially designated minorities. International organizations, in particular the Council of Europe and the European Community, are now showing considerable interest in the treatment suffered by Gypsies in the various member states and are making fresh recommendations and proposals. In some states, a dialogue has begun between representatives of Gypsy organizations and the government. There is some hope, for it seems possible that regulations may be changed and that Gypsies might at last be considered as having a recognized culture, no longer referred to as 'Travelling People' or 'persons of nomadic origin'. In December 1981, for example, a French cabinet minister visited two campsites near Paris. In his speech he said that the government would break with the earlier policy of settlement and assimilation and would look at changes in the regulations, in an effort to develop sources of income that would assure independence, in the framework of respect for a culture that would receive recognition and protection.

The French government therefore seems to be moving from negative actions to positive words. But as always, it remains to be seen whether the fine words will be followed by action.

'Freedom, too, must be organized,' the French minister said in his speech. And therein lies one of the difficulties on the road to cultural pluralism. The modern state will have to legislate who has the right to be different and who will have the resources to remain different. Appropriate regulations might turn the right to be different into the obligation to be different. Fake respect for a kind of difference that is accepted only when it becomes folklore and is properly regulated may prove to be the last incarnation of an assimilationist policy. Will state organs take it upon themselves to define Gypsy culture by proxy, thus making Gypsies bear the burden of the morbid nostalgia of a culture that feels so lost itself that it seizes upon other 'minority' or 'community' cultures, while simultaneously accelerating their disappearance? The renewal of interest in 'small groups', the notion that 'small is beautiful', encourages infatuation with 'minorities'.

The Gypsies, like many other minorities, are highly market-able these days. The fashion for Gypsies has now become a feature of the environment in which they live. This threat to turn their culture into spectacle is a danger more difficult to apprehend than the effects of the various regulations or of social work and schooling. There is now a risk that lack of respect will give way to pseudo-respect. In some ways this is worse, because it is garbed in an insincerity and 'fraternalism' that are more dangerous than the paternalism that preceded it.

Gypsies do not fall into the usual categories. They are neither Third World nor Fourth World, they are not immigrant work-ers, they yearn for no country of origin and have no country to go back to. There are few appropriate 'institutional responses' to them. Some of the questions now being put to Gypsies and their organizations amount to asking what sauce they would like to be devoured with. Some sections of the Gypsy populations need aid, but not guidance; technical and social assistance is what is required, but it is the latter that is being expanded. The re-cipient of this kind of aid becomes more dependent. It may prove to be true, as André Glucksmann has observed, that 'irrespective of ideologies, for a millennium now, the call to "eliminate ghettos" has actually been a call to eliminate those who live in them'. Changing the regulations will not automatic-ally change the centuries-old attitude of rejection by the local populace and local authorities. Nor will stereotypes fade over-night—not when the present situation is the outcome of six centuries of history.

While in principle states can do much for the cause of the Gypsy people, it would be dangerous for the Gypsies to expect too much of them. Gypsies must rely on themselves above all, and on the determination that is growing with their organizations. The kaleidoscopic variety of the Gypsy populations has so far stymied the all-embracing assimilation policies, and while Gypsies have thus forced their environment to recognize some limits, this era is now drawing to a close. The consequent sense of urgency is one of the reasons why, for the first time in their history, Gypsies are emerging from their invisibility and openly opposing their enemies.

Gypsies have almost always been seen as foreign rather than as foreigners, their alien character being more social than racial or cultural. Recent policies consider them deviants to be 're-integrated'. Present-day humanism therefore grants Gypsies a great deal as individuals, but very little as a community. The Gypsy organizations are seeking to reverse this trend, insisting that it is the community that counts. This is, in fact, a tradition of their social organization: Gypsies cannot exist alone, and the group as a whole disappears if it does not keep a tenuous balance through flexibility. The repeated denials of their culture ultimately represent negative proof of its existence: those who seek to deny it merely emphasize the reality they seek to erase. Whichever group they belong to, Gypsies and Travellers find themselves bound together indifferently in the image others have of them, and they all suffer the consequences of this image. The unity that the Gypsy organizations are seeking to create is thus formed from the outside to some extent. Gypsies are not asking for charity or paternalism. They do not want to be considered victims or parasites. They simply wish to live in a style that deserves respect, without having to go from galley-slavery to the bondage of the assembly line.

Fundamentally, what Gypsies want is to continue to live their lives in peace and independence, without having endlessly to defend themselves. Gypsy society, scorned by so many outsiders, has forged a deep-rooted strength among its members. One thinks of the allegory in a Yugoslav film, *Who's That Singing Over There?*, directed by Slobodan Sijan. Some young Gypsies, travelling with other people in an old bus, are harassed by their fellow passengers. But the bus is later caught in a bomb attack, and the Gypsies are much better able than the others to face difficulties and overcome fear. They take out their musical instruments and begin to sing. It had seemed they were weaker,

Keeping history alive

Three Gypsy men

they turn out to be stronger; they stay calm through the turmoil, and in the end are the only ones to survive.

But others make them doubt their strength: 'They are afraid of being naive. Deep down they are not sure whether their way of life is evidence of a gift or a manifestation of weakness' [9, p. 220], and they sometimes end up blaming themselves for their plight:

> I see that our Manuš have nothing to envy all the other Manuš. It's unbelievable how smart they can be! But what the hell do they all want with a regular cage? They may as well just ask for a zoo! *Kamlo Devel* [Dear God]! All this stupidity and naïvety is driving me crazy. Some day we'll all be wearing numbers on our lapels, and everyone will cheer, us first of all. This may sound cynical, but I'm happy that the gadže reject us, because that way the gadže are unwittingly giving us the chance not to fall into stationary settlement. But we, fools that we are, rush in head-first. Lord, where are the *rabouins* [devils] of the old days? All gone, or just about. I admit, every people has the right to evolve, to free itself of the shackles of the past. But with us it's the other way around, we make our own chains . . . Whose fault is it? Ours? Society's? In my opinion, it's a little bit everybody's fault, or maybe it's just fate, and we're doomed to sink without a trace by the year 2000.

Modern caravan drawn by horses

One day I read somewhere that one of our ancestors is supposed to have made the nails used to crucify Jesus Christ, the Son of God, and that after this 'good deed' the whole world cursed him. Then he was damned and banished from the face of the earth, him and all his family and descendants (namely us). My personal epilogue to the story: God says to His son: 'You've been punishing them for nineteen centuries, that's enough already. I, your father, order you to take a rest, my son, because now it's my turn. I condemn them to nineteen centuries of settlement, and after these nineteen centuries of wandering that you gave them, it isn't going to be easy. Good luck to them. Concrete will give them all the psychological disorders they need, imaginary ailments and so on. Don't worry, my son, get some rest, papa's taking over now. Thus your revenge endures.' (Correspondence, 1982.)

Will the Gypsies wind up in ghettos, in reservations where, like an endangered species, they can wander and reproduce while putting on displays of folklore for others? Or will their organizations enable them to preserve the flexibility and invisibility that have protected their independence so far?

It will probably not be too long before we can tell whether the twilight of the Gypsies is leading to a new dawn or to a long dark night.

BIBLIOGRAPHY

[1] Acton, T., *Gypsy Politics and Social Change*, Routledge & Kegan Paul, London 1974.

[2] Adams, B., Okely, J., Morgan, D., Smith, D., *Gypsies and Government Policy in England*, Heinemann, Centre for Environmental Studies, 1975.

[3] Amid, *Dictionnaire persan*, Librairie Evicene, 1958.

[4] Andersen, R. E., 'Symbolism, Symbiosis and Survival: Roles of Young Women of the Kalderaša in Philadelphia', in M. T. Salo (ed.) *The American Kalderaš: Gypsies in the New World*, Gypsy Lore Society, North American Chapter, Centenary College, Hacketts-town 1981.

[5] *Archivo de la Corona de Aragón*, 12 January 1425, safe-conduct issued to 'don Johan de Egipte Menor'.

[6] Asseo, H., 'Le traitement administratif des Bohémiens au xviie siècle', in *Problèmes socio-culturels en France au xviie siècle*, Kincksieck 1975.

[7] Asseo, H., 'L'histoire', in J.-P. Liégeois (ed.), *Les populations tsiganes en France*, ministère de l'Education nationale, Centre de recherches tsiganes, 1981.

[8] Bataillard, P., 'De l'apparition et de la dispersion des Bohémiens en Europe', *Bibliothèque de l'Ecole des Chartes*, v, 1843–1844, pp. 348–75 and 521–52.

[9] Bazin, H., *Les Bienheureux de la Desolation*, le Seuil, 1970.

[10] Baudrimont, A., *Vocabulaire de la langue des Bohémiens habitant les pays basques français*, Bordeaux 1862.

[11] Belloni, K., 'Témoignages', in J.-P Liégeois (ed.), *Les Populations tsiganes en France*, ministère de l'Education nationale, Centre de recherches tsiganes, 1981.

[12] Belon, P., *Les Observations de plusieurs singularitez et choses mémorables trouvées en Grèce, Asie, Judée, Egypte, Arabie et autres pays estranges*, Paris 1553.

[13] Bernadac, C., *L'Holocauste oublié, le massacre des Tsiganes*, France-Empire, 1979.

Bibliography

[14] Bernard, M., and Chatard, R. P., *Zanko, chef tribal*, le Vieux Colombier, Paris 1959.
[15] Beti, M., 'Identité et tradition', in G. Michaud, *Négritude, traditions et développement*, Complexe, 1979.
[16] Bilmans, M., 'Situation juridique des Rom en Europe occidentale', *Romano Kongreso*, Geneva, April 1978.
[17] Bloch, J., *Les Tsiganes*, PUF, 1953.
[18] Block, M., *Gypsies: Their Life and Their Customs* (tr. B. Kuczynski and D. Taylor), Methuen and Co., London 1938.
[19] Borde, A., *Fyrste Boke of the Introduction of Knowledge*, London 1542.
[20] Bordigoni, M., *La Scolarisation des enfants tsiganes de l'agglomération marseillaise*, mémoire de sociologie, université de Provence, 1980.
[21] Calvet, G., 'La langue' in J.-P. Liégeois (ed.), *Les Populations tsiganes en France*, ministère de l'Education nationale, Centre de recherches tsiganes, 1981.
[22] Calvo Buezas, T., 'Las minorías etnicas y sus relaciones de clase, raza, y etnía' in *Los Gitanos en la Sociedad española*, Documentación social, no. 41, Cáritas, Madrid 1980.
[23] Cannizo, M., *D'où viens-tu Gitan?*, mémoire pour le CAEI d'instituteur, 1980.
[24] Castan, N., 'La justice expéditive', *Annales*, no. 2, 1976.
[25] Childers, C. H., 'Banjaras', in L. S. Leshnik and G. D. Sondheimer, *Pastoralists and Nomads in South-Asia*, Otto Harrassowitz, Wiesbaden 1975, pp. 247–65.
[26] Clébert, J.-P., *The Gypsies* (tr. C. Duff), Penguin, 1967; new edition *Les Tsiganes*, Tchou, 1976.
[27] Colinon, M., *Des inconnus parmi nous, les Gitans*, SPES, 1968.
[28] Covarrubias, S., *Tesoro de la lengua castellana o española*, Madrid 1611.
[29] Cripps, J., *Accommodation for Gypsies*, Department of the Environment and Welsh Office, HMSO, 1976.
[30] Crofton, H. T., 'Borde's Egipt speech, *Journal of the Gypsy Lore Society*, 1.
[31] Crofton, H. T., 'Early Annals of the Gypsies in England', *Journal of the Gypsy Lore Society*, 1.
[32] Daval, M. and Joly, D., 'La langue des Tsiganes' in *Les Tsiganes en Alsace*, Strasbourg 1979.
[33] David, M., 'Réflexions sur l'avenir commercial des voyageurs', in *Etudes tsiganes*, no. 4, 1974.
[34] Davidova, E., 'The Gypsies in Czechoslovakia' in *Journal of the Gypsy Lore Society*, (3) XLIX, 3–4.
[35] Davidova, E. and Guy, D. E., 'Czechoslovakia and her Gypsies' in T. Acton (ed.), *Current changes among British Gypsies and their place in international patterns of development*, Oxford 1971.
[36] Delaunay, C., *Django, mon frère*, Losfeld 1968.
[37] Digard, J.-P., 'Tsiganes et pasteurs nomades dans le sud-ouest de

Bibliography

l'Iran', *in* J.-P. Liégeois (ed.), *Tsiganes et nomades, tendances actuelles de la recherche*, Hommes et Migrations, Paris 1978.

[38] Ely, B., 'L'anthropologie des Tsiganes', *Etudes tsiganes*, no. 1, 1960.

[39] *Enciclopedia Universal Ilustrada*, vol. 26, Espasa-Calpe, Madrid 1925.

[40] Formoso, B., *Niglo, aspects économiques des rapports interpersonnels chez les Tsiganes*, mémoire de DEA, Ecole des hautes études en sciences sociales, 1982.

[41] Foucault, M., *Discipline and Punish, The Birth of the Prison* (tr. A. Sheridan), Allen Lane, London 1977.

[42] Fraser, A. M., 'The Travellers: Developments in England and Wales, 1953–1963', *Journal of The Gypsy Lore Society*, (3), vol. XLIII.

[43] Frere, J.-C., *L'Enigme des Gitans*, Mam, 1973, collection 'Pensées et sociétés secrètes'.

[44] Garassus, F., *La Doctrine curieuse des beaux esprits de ce temps ou pretendus téls . . .*, Paris 1623.

[45] Gentleman, H., Swift, S., *Scotland's Travelling People: Problems and Solutions*, HMSO, Edinburgh 1971.

[46] Gentleman, H., 'The Scottish Development department and the travelling people in Scotland', in T. Acton (ed.) *Current changes among British Gypsies and their place in international patterns of development*, National Gypsy Education Council, 1971.

[47] Gjerdman, O., and Ljungberg, E., *The Language of the Swedish Coppersmith Gypsy Johan Dimitri Taikon*, Uppsala 1963.

[48] Grellmann, H. M. Gottlieb, *Die Zigeuner, Ein historischer Versuch über die Lebensart und Verfassung . . .* Dessau and Leipzig 1783.

[49] Gropper, R. C., *Gypsies in the City*, Darwin Press, 1975.

[50] Gropper, R. C., 'What does blood tell?', *Newsletter of the Gypsy Lore Society*, vol. 4, no. 2 et seq., Hackettstown, New Jersey, 1981.

[51] Guy, W., 'Ways of looking at Roms: the Case of Czechoslovakia', in F. Rehfisch (ed.) *Gypsies, Tinkers and Other Travellers*, Academic Press, 1975.

[52] *Gypsies and other Travellers*, Ministry of Housing and Local Government, HMSO, 1967.

[53] Haesler, W., *Enfants de la grand-route*, Delachaux and Niestlé 1955.

[54] Hancock, I. F. (ed.) *Romani Sociolinguistics*, special issue of *International Journal of the Sociology of Language*, no. 19, Mouton 1979.

[55] Hermann, 'Little Egypt', *Journal of the Gypsy Lore Society*, (1), vol. III, 1891, pp. 152–5.

[56] Hoess, R., *Commandant of Auschwitz: The autobiography of R. Hoess* (tr. C. Fitzgibbon), Pan Books, London 1961.

[57] Horvathova, E., *Cigáni na Slovensku*, Bratislava 1964, summary in English.

[58] Hubschmannova, M., *Notes about the position of Gypsies-Rom in*

Czechoslovakia, Institute of Sociology of the Academy of Sciences, Prague n.d.

[59] Hubschmannova, M., 'Langage des Rom en Tchécoslovaquie', *Etudes tsiganes*, no. 1, 1978.

[60] Hubschmannova, M., 'What can sociology suggest about the origin of Roms?' *Archiv Orientalni*, 40 (1), 1972, pp. 51–64.

[61] Jochimsen, L., *Zigeuner heute*, Ferdinand Enke Verlag, Stuttgart 1963.

[62] *Journal d'un bourgeois de Paris*, anonymous chronicle, 1405–1449, published by Alexandre Tuetey, Paris 1881.

[63] Kenrick, D., and Puxon, G., *The Destiny of Europe's Gypsies*, Chatto-Heinemann, 1972.

[64] Kenrick, D. and Acton, T., *Le Statut juridique des Tsiganes en Grande-Bretagne*, mimeo, 1977.

[65] Lafuente, R., *Los gitanos, el flamenco y los flamencos*, Barna, Barcelona 1955.

[66] Le Trosne, G., *Mémoire sur les vagabonds*, 1764.

[67] Liégeois, J.-P., 'Veillée gitane', *Etudes tsiganes*, no. 3, 1967.

[68] Liégeois, J.-P., *Les Tsiganes*, le Seuil, 1971.

[69] Liégeois, J.-P., *Mutation tsigane*, PUF, 1976.

[70] Liégeois, J.-P., 'Le nomade', preface to G. Rondeau, *Scènes de la vie tsigane*, ed. Astrid, 1982.

[71] Liégeois, J.-P., *Gypsies and Travellers*, Council of Europe, 1985.

[72] Lopez de Meneses, A., 'La immigración gitana en España en el siglo xv', in *Martinez Ferrando Achivero*, Asociación nacional de bibliotecarios, archiveros y archeologos, 1968.

[73] Luna, J.-C., de, *Gitanos de la Bética*, EPESA, Madrid 1951.

[74] Macritchie, D., *The Gypsies of India*, Delhi 1886 (and 1976).

[75] Manzano, R., *Cante Jondo*, Barna, Barcelona n.d.

[76] Maria, R., 'Les Tsiganes dans la Tchécoslovaquie d'aujourd' hui', *Etudes tsiganes*, no. 4, 1966.

[77] Matzen, R., 'Les emprunts des manouches d'Alsace à l'allemand et à l'alsacien', *Saisons d'Alsace*, Strasbourg, no. 67, 1979.

[78] Meile, P., 'Observations sur la langue tsigane', *Etudes tsiganes*, no. 1, 1955.

[79] Mode, H., Wolffling, S., *Zigeuner: der Weg eines Volkes in Deutschland*, Koehler und Amelang, Leipzig 1968.

[80] Moncada, S., de, *Restauración politica de España, y Deseos Públicos, que escrivió en ocho Discursos el Doctor Sancho de Moncada*, Madrid 1619.

[81] Morel, O., *La Vie à Châtillon-en-Dombes d'après les comptes des syndics*, vol. ii, Bourg, 1927, doc. cc9, Account of 1418–1419, 22 August, 1419.

[82] Münster, S., *La Cosmographie universelle de tout le monde, augmentée, ornée et enrichie par François de Belleforest*, Paris 1575.

[83] Muratori, L. A., 'Cinganorum adventus in Italiam', 1422, in

Bibliography

Rerum Italicarum Scriptores, vol. 18–611–612 published in 1731, reprinted by F. Dyrlund, *Tatere og Natmands-Folk i Danmark . . .* Copenhagen 1872, pp. 362–4.

[84] Novitch, M., 'Le génocide des Tsiganes sous le régime nazi', *Revue de l'Association des médecins israélites de France*, no. 164, March 1968.

[85] Okely, J., 'Gypsy Women: Models in Conflict', in S. Ardener (ed.), *Perceiving Women*, Malaby Press, 1975.

[86] Palmireno, L., *El Estudioso Cortesano*, Alcala de Henares, 1587.

[87] Piasere, L., 'Il sistema di parentela e il parentado cognatico dei Rom Xoraxané', *l'Uomo*, vol. IV. no. 1, 1980.

[88] Piasere, L., 'La terminologie des parents consanguins chez deux groupes rom', *Etudes tsiganes*, no. 2, 1982.

[89] Piasere, L., *Māre Roma: catégories humaines et structure sociale. Une Contribution à l'ethnologie tsigane*, Etudes et Documents Balkaniques et Mediterranéens, no. 8, Collège de France, Paris 1985.

[90] Pittard, E., *Les Tsiganes ou Bohémiens: Recherches anthropologiques dans la peninsule des Balkans*, Geneva 1932.

[91] Plancy, C., de, *Dictionnaire infernal*, Paris 1845.

[92] Pott, A. F., *Die Zigeuner in Europa und Asien*, Halle 1844.

[93] Pottinger, Sir H., *Travels in Beloutchistan and Sinde*, London 1816.

[94] Predari, F., *Origine e vicende dei zingari con documenti intorno alle propietà fisiche e morali . . .*, Lampato, Milan 1841.

[95] Puxon, G., *On the Road*, National Council for Civil Liberties, 1968.

[96] Puxon, G., *Rom: Europe's Gypsies*, Minority Rights Group report, no. 14, London 1973.

[97] Ramirez Heredie, J. de Dios, *Nosotros los Gitanos*, Ediciones 29.

[98] Rao, A., *Les Qorbat: contribution à l'étude économique et sociale d'un groupe Jat d'Afghanistan*, thesis, University of Paris IV, 1979.

[99] *Report of the Department Committee on Vagrancy in Scotland*, 1936.

[100] Rinderknecht, K., 'Les Tsiganes en Suisse', in *Tsiganes, nomades mystérieux*, Mondo, 1973.

[101] Roberts, S., *The Gypsies: their origin, continuance, and destinations, as clearly foretold in the prophecies of Isaiah, Jeremiah and Ezekiel*, London 1836.

[102] *Roma-Weltkongress und Sinti-Alltag*, Pressespiegel III, Universität Bremen, 1982.

[103] Rudiger, J. C., *Von der Sprache und Herkunft der Zigeuner aus Indien*, Leipzig and Halle 1782.

[104] Salo, M. T., 'The Expression of Ethnicity in Rom Oral Tradition', *Western Folklore*, vol. XXXVI, no. 1, 1977.

[105] Salo, M. T., 'Kalderaš economic organization' in M. T. Salo (ed.), *The American Kalderaš: Gypsies in the New World*, Gypsy Lore Society, North American Chapter, Centenary College, Hacketts-town 1981.

[106] Sampson, J., 'Gypsy language and origin', *Journal of the Gypsy Lore Society*, (2), vol. I, 1907–1908.

[107] Sampson, J., 'On the Origins and early Migrations of the Gypsies', *Journal of the Gypsy Lore Society*, (3), vol. II, 1923.

[108] Sampson, J., *The Dialect of the Gypsies of Wales, being the older form of British Romani*, Oxford 1926.

[109] *Scharotl*, The Newspaper of travelling people in Switzerland, Bern 1976.

[110] Serboianu, P., *Les Tsiganes*, Payot, 1930.

[111] Silverman, C., 'Pollution and power: Gypsy women in America', in M. T. Salo (ed.), *The American Kalderaš: Gypsies in the New World*, Gypsy Lore Society, North American Chapter, Centenary College, Hackettstown 1981.

[112] Soravia, G., 'Vocabulario sinto delle Venezie', in *Lacio drom* no. 4–5, Rome 1981.

[113] Suchel, J., *Situation des Tsiganes sous la législation actuelle en Tchécoslovaquie et en Angleterre*, Ministry of Labour and Social Affairs, Prague n.d.

[114] Sutherland, A., *Gypsies: the Hidden Americans*, Tavistock, London 1975.

[115] Sutherland, A., 'The American Rom: A Case of Economic Adaptation', in F. Rehfisch, *Gypsies, Tinkers and Other Travellers*, Academic Press, 1975.

[116] Taikon, K., in *Zigenaren*, review of Gypsies in Sweden, no. 1–2, 1967.

[117] Taylor, G., 'The problem of poverty 1660–1834' in *Seminar Studies in History*, Longman, London 1969.

[118] Tipler, D., 'Les Gitans en Amérique du Nord', *Monde gitan*, no. 11.

[119] *Towards Gypsy Power*, Romanestan Publications, mimeo, London 1977.

[120] Turner, R. L., 'The Position of the Romany in Indo-Aryan', *Journal of the Gypsy Lore Society* (3), vol. V (1926) and VI (1927).

[121] Tyrnauer, G., 'Mastering the Past: Germans and Gypsies', in J. N. Porter (ed.), *Genocide and Human Rights: A Global Anthology*, University Press of America, 1982.

[122] Vaillant, J.-A., *Les Rômes, histoire vraie des vrais Bohémiens*, new edition 1979.

[123] Vallières, J. des, *Le Chevalier de Camargue*, 1956.

[124] Valtonen, P., *Suomen Mustalaiskielen Etymologinen Sanakirja*, Helsinki 1972.

[125] Van Kappen, O., *Geschiedenis der Zigeuners in Nederland*, Assen 1965.

[126] Van Kappen, O., 'Histoire des Tsiganes aux Pays-Bas. L'évolution du status des "Paiens" ou "Egyptiens" dans les Pays-Bas du Nord (1420–1750)', in *Acta Historiae Neerlandica* III, Leiden 1968.

[127] Van Kappen, O., 'A Prague edict against Gypsies', *Journal of the Gypsy Lore Society* (3) XLII, 3–4.

[128] Varnagy, E., 'Les problèmes sociaux des enfants tsiganes en Hongrie', in J.-P. Liégeois (ed.) *Tsiganes et nomades, tendances actuelles de la recherche*, Hommes et Migrations, 1978.

[129] Vaux de Foletier, F. de., *Les Tsiganes dans l'ancienne France*, Connaissance du Monde, Paris 1961.

[130] Vaux de Foletier, F. de, 'Le pèlerinage romain des Tsiganes en 1422 et les lettres du pape Martin v' in *Etudes tsiganes*, no. 4, 1965.

[131] Vaux de Foletier, F. de, *Mille Ans d'histoire des Tsiganes*, Fayard, 1970.

[132] Vaux de Foletier, F. de, 'Un recensement des Tsiganes de Bavière en 1905', in *Etudes tsiganes*, no. 3, 1978.

[133] Vaux de Foletier, F. de, *Les Bohémiens en France au XIXᵉ siècle*, Lattès, 1981.

[134] Voetius, G., *Selectarum disputationum . . .*, Utrecht 1655 to 1669.

[135] Vulcanius, B., *De literis et lingua Getarum sive Gothorum . . .*, Leiden, 1597.

[136] Wagenseil, J.-C., *De . . . civitate Noribergensi commentario . . .*, Altdorfi 1697.

[137] Wellers, G., 'La propagande néo-nazie et l'extermination des Juifs et des Tsiganes', *Rencontre, Chrétiens et Juifs*, no. 59, 1979.

[138] Wiesenthal, S., Speech at the International Gypsy Congress at Göttingen, 16 May 1981.

[139] Williams, P., 'La société', in J.-P. Liégeois (ed.), *Les Populations tsiganes en France*, ministère de l'Education nationale, Centre de recherches tsiganes, 1981.

[140] Williams, P., *Une ceremonie de demande en mariage dans une communauté tsigane*, SELAF, Paris, 1983.

[141] Winsted, E. O., 'The Gypsies of Modon and the "Wye of Romeney"', in *Journal of the Gypsy Lore Society* (2), vol. III, 1909.